MW00464856

A Touch of the Infinite

Infinite

Studies in Music Appreciation
with Charlotte Mason

Megan Hoyt

POWERHOUSE PRESS

A Touch of the Infinite
© 2016 Powerhouse Press

ISBN: ISBN-13:
978-0692530412

ISBN-10:
069253041X

Edited by Timothy Laurio
Designed by Helen Weigt

Powerhouse Press
9111 Brocklehurst Ln
Charlotte, NC 28215
+1 704 453 1408
www.meganhoyt.net
www.powerhousepress.weebly.com/

Printed in the United States of America.

There is no satisfaction for the Soul of a man, save one, because the things about him are finite, measurable, incomplete; and his reach is beyond his grasp; he has an urgent, incessant, irrepressible need of the infinite.

—Charlotte Mason, *Ourselves*

In honor of my parents, Michael and Nancy Glass,
who unknowingly awakened a passion for
orchestral music within this
frail and fragile child.

ff

In this great work, we seek and assuredly find the co-operation of the Divine Spirit, whom we recognise, in a sense rather new to modern thought, as the Supreme Educator of mankind in things that have been called secular, fully as much as in those that have been called sacred.

—Charlotte Mason, *Parents and Children*

Table of Contents

Acknowledgements

Where does one begin to acknowledge the people, past and present, who ignited within you this passion for music and for life? It began with my parents, Michael and Nancy Glass, and spread to their orchestra friends who welcomed me backstage at odd hours with open arms. The stagehands were also great friends, orchestra manager Will Roberts always had an extra smile for me, Mary K Holder Glass, Jean Colford, Audrey Anastasi, Bob and Lois Vornholt, Mimi McShane, Milo Deering, and my father's dear friend Henry Mancini all impacted my love for music.

I'm especially thankful for my fellow Charlotte Mason enthusiasts: the amazing Leslie Laurio, Timothy Laurio, Hannah Hoyt, Hilary Herndon, Drew Hoyt, Jesse Hoyt, Steven Hoyt, Karen Glass, Anne White, Wendi Capehart, Donna Jean Breckenridge, Lynn Bruce, Jeanne Webb, Tammy Glaser, Deborah Miller, Jennifer Gagnon, Laurie Bestvater, Melanie Walker-Malone, and Helen Weigt. Your support and care kept the dream alive, and your friendship continues to nourish my soul.

Acknowledgements

Introduction

It is incontestable that music induces in us a sense of the infinite and the contemplation of the invisible.

—*Victor de Laprade*

We chose to educate our family at home, using the guiding principles of Charlotte Mason to navigate the murky places and trusting in our relationship with God, the Creator of this vast universe of ours, to make our days fruitful. At times, it felt as if our family's educational journey was etched with pure gold. Something new enchanted us every single day—either a poem or a song, a new work of fiction, the reward of learning a new math concept or watching mourning doves' nest outside an upstairs window, the beauty of a field of wildflowers waving in the breeze on a fragrant spring day. Those of us who have chosen this educational path have found a glorious way of living for our families, and I would very much like to share this paradigm shift of ours with you.

We began by following the tenets of Miss Charlotte Maria Shaw Mason, a woman who never married or had children of her own. I am sure the irony of this situation was not lost on God. He probably couldn't wait to see the looks on our faces after He poured knowledge and wisdom about the education of children into one we would never predict would be the receiver—Miss Mason, a fragile orphan with tenuous health, no money, and few prospects, but lots of heart. It seems almost obvious in light of who Jesus chose as disciples that this humble woman would be God's vessel, the one to receive His whispers of educational wisdom. We should have expected it.

In her third volume, *School Education*, Miss Mason said, "Our part is to remove obstructions and to give stimulus and guidance to the child who is trying to get into touch with the universe of things and thoughts which belongs to him."[1] We quietly urge toward right living while supplying quality materials and books to our beloved children so that they will have access to "a universe of things and thoughts." They form objects out of clay, build birdhouses, examine beehives and cocoons, paint pictures of nature specimens, carve things out of wood, memorize beautiful poems, sing hymns and folk songs, learn to play an instrument and enjoy the great paintings, sculptures, architecture, and music of the past.

This life is glorious, isn't it? All of this—the entire universe of living ideas—belongs to every human being. I hope one day we can provide each child in our midst with a feast of living ideas. I pray it will happen soon. The world is in desperate need of this universe of thoughts and things. We pine for them and fill our lives with busyness because they are missing. And most of us don't even realize what it is we're pining for.

While Miss Mason did not reference composer study regularly in her volumes on educational method, she did leave us with a list of books included in her PNEU programmes (Parents National Educational Union) and with a few wise admonitions—one of which was to trust in the lessons of Annie Jessy Curwen, who you will meet within these pages. You will also hear from Mr. and Mrs. Cedric Howard Glover, Percy Alfred Scholes, Arthur Pollitt, Emma Marshall, Sir Hubert Parry, and Marjorie Ransom, among others. We will glean what we can from these trusted music mentors Miss Mason left to us as we formulate a plan for studying the great composers of the past.

I should not have been, but I was surprised (in a good way) to learn that each book Miss Mason chose for composer study and music education was littered with those same thoughts and principles she placed within her volumes: the importance of relationship, the value of ideas over dry facts, the use of story to engage a child's mind with the subject at hand. She did not leave us a "how to" manual, but here is one thing we do know—Miss Mason trusted Cedric Howard Glover to gather a series of articles by various authors and educators, articles that appeared in the *Parents' Review*, and publish them in book form. This book, *The Term's Music*, is one of the few we can directly attribute to the oversight of Miss Mason. Within its pages are the thoughts she approved, the ideas she espoused.

Here is a quotation from the introduction to *The Term's Music*:

> People cannot be taught to appreciate good music, unless they have
> first learnt to discriminate between good music and bad. It is not
> enough just to play them good music, unless at the same time we can
> awaken that finer sense, which will enable them to determine why it is
> good. There is an absolute standard of good in music as inexorable as
> any ethical standard. ... The object therefore of the instruction, with
> which this book is concerned, should be to foster the natural good taste
> of the subject, and gradually to build up a fund of experience, which
> may serve as a standard of right and wrong, incidentally bringing him
> into contact with some of the great creative geniuses of the world and
> providing him with a treasure house of beautiful things, which will be
> a joy to him all his life.[2]

Before we look at the books Miss Mason used or the exam questions or any
of the other juicy things I have in store for you, we should at the outset identify
what her music study looked like. Here it is in summary, again excerpted from
The Term's Music:

> The natural corollary is that all children, whether "musical" or
> "unmusical," should receive some general instruction in music and
> that such instruction should ideally be given as an ordinary lesson in
> the regular curriculum and not as an extra subject. In actual practice
> this ideal is probably rarely attainable, as the ordinary instructor is
> at present insufficiently equipped for the purpose. In any case, the
> instruction should be a regular weekly occurrence and not limited by
> the occasional visit at irregular intervals of an outside music teacher.
> The music lesson will naturally fall into several divisions. At least
> one quarter of the time available should be devoted to Ear Training.
> Mr. F.H. Shera's Musical Groundwork (Milford, 3. 6d.) is strongly
> recommended for this purpose; it consists of a progressive course of
> lessons for each term and is written in a manner comprehensible to
> expert or tyro [novice] alike, being therefore particularly suitable for
> those who have to train themselves preparatory to training their pupils.

After the ear training exercises are completed, a short space of time should be devoted to acquainting the pupils with the rudiments of music--the meaning of the commonest musical terms, the instruments of the orchestra, illustrated by the H.M.V., records D.555 to 558 (each 6s. 6d.) and such like. The information imported should be of a severely practical nature, such as is contained in Mr. Percy Scholes' excellent handbooks for listeners to music, care being taken not to burden the minds of the pupils with lists of technical terms, which have too general application; attention should be focused chiefly on such things as the historical growth of the different musical forms, the evolution of the orchestra and the keyboard instruments, not on the nomenclature of chords or the different species of counterpoint. The remainder of the time available should be devoted to studying the composer of the term.[3]

That's not a bit intimidating, is it? We will unpack Glover's advice mentioned above one tiny morsel at a time. Meanwhile, let's rest in the knowledge that God has brought us to this place and will surely not allow us to fail in our quest—our thirst—for musical knowledge and skill and for a large room in which to set our children, the largest in the House of Mind that we can afford and the choicest feast we can manage to spread for them.

Miss Mason said the purpose of education "should be to lead a child into the fullest, truest, noblest and most fruitful relations of which he is capable, with the world in which he lives."[4] This book is my humble attempt to help teachers not only understand the methods of Charlotte Mason as applied to music study but to show children how to enjoy true, noble, and fruitful relationships with music, with its ultimate Creator, and with those anointed men and women of genius who cooperated with the Divine Spirit to bring us the rich music we spread at the feast.

Introduction

A touch of the Infinite

To the Teacher: But for you, if you are ambitious and alive with interest for your work, there is a promising art-soil throughout the length and breadth of this big land of ours, from which a rich harvest may be reaped, provided a healthy seed be planted with care and the young shoot thence watched and nurtured with intelligence, faith and enthusiasm.

—Maud Powell, "The American Girl and Her Violin"

Chapter One

Our Reason for the Journey:
The Divine Intention

It is as revealers of God to their children that parents touch their highest limitations; perhaps it is only as they succeed in this part of their work that they fulfill the Divine intention in giving them children to bring up—in the nurture and admonition of the Lord.

—Charlotte Mason, *Parents and Children*

L ife is full of tiny moments flush with joy that catch us up in their beauty. We are moved by a beautiful song, a lovely painting, a sweet fragrance, or even the smooth touch of a gentle rose petal on our skin. We need only to adjust our inner antennae—a lean-in here toward inspiration and joy and a tiny shove there away from cynicism and doubt—to fully experience the almost tangible magnificence of this life. Yet, surrounded by diapers and duties, the urge to pop on the latest animated feature just for a moment's respite from the responsibilities of parenthood is ever present. We have to consciously force *ourselves* to tune in to the child in front of us and tune out the pressures and pace of the world around us in order to reach for that glimpse of joy.

American society's idea of progress and its mad dash for success have left me parched and thirsty for something more, something different, something other than life in the technological age. At the same time, a computer with access to every TV show and every movie ever made and available at any time is always tempting me to step outside of real life and into passive entertainment. I'm not even talking about twaddle here. They could be worthwhile documentaries or historical dramas vying for my attention, but whenever I watch instead of actively seeking relationship with people and things in the real world, I know I am not fully living. Has it been the same for you?

We must be present in the moment to find this joy, and I don't think many twenty-first century Americans are completely present. The pace of life must slow if we are to see, hear, and feel in any true way. This decision to stop and smell the roses (sometimes literally) should begin in childhood, according to Miss Mason. This kind of slow savoring of thoughts and ideas, this tentative enjoyment of the natural world (dare we allow *ourselves* the luxury when we should be keeping busy?) is one of the many ideas about life that we need to transmit to our children, because it is much easier when learned in childhood. As a child, I gradually recognized certain vague notions that nipped at me over the course of time. Slowing the pace of life and stopping to ponder the meaning of the world around me was one of those notions. Slowly savoring the beauty around us can help us think large thoughts and allow us to ask giant questions of ourselves, if we will only stand still long enough to form them:

- Is there really a God Who created the universe with one magnificent Word?
- What does it mean to be holy and noble?
- What is base and crude and unacceptable to me?
- What is beautiful and true?

We formulate theories as children—ideas with opaque edges that gradually take shape, becoming solid and dependable within the framework of our daily lives as we grow older. We immerse *ourselves* in these living ideas, sometimes becoming drenched with their fervor and intensity and other times tolerating only a sprinkling here and there. "A soul awoke within a water-sprite at the touch of love," Miss Mason says, and we believe her because our souls were so awakened once we began devouring her volumes and embarking on this journey toward real living. It happens in starts and stops at first, but eventually our inclinations toward beauty, truth, and goodness prevail and a love of noble and high-minded thinking becomes second nature to us.

Music is more than merely the backdrop of all these living ideas we are now slowing down long enough to ponder. It can be the vehicle with which we impress them upon our children, not in a rote way but naturally, over time. Music is the essence of inspiration itself; it is proof positive of the existence of God. We are inspired by the inherent genius of a great master such as Beethoven or Bach, and we recognize that true genius comes from above, from the Father of Lights. We are awed. We stand aside and bow before His glory, tears streaming, as we listen to Beethoven's symphonies, realizing that in the composer's feeble state, this great gift could not have been entirely his.

May Byron, in her book *A Day with Ludwig van Beethoven*, says:

> ... the Adagio from his great Quartet in C Sharp Minor is in itself a prayer, a period of conference with God, in faith, in eternal goodness. [quoting Wagner] And it was in a state of mind which one may term unconsciously devotional, that the great composer now ascended into regions where few could follow him, where, his senses deaf and blind to earthly sights and sounds, he could hold intercourse with a pure and celestial Heaven.[5]

We receive the same glimpse of Heaven as we listen to the hymns of Fanny Crosby. Blind almost from birth, she wrote over nine thousand hymns to the glory of God, and this is what she had to say about her affliction:

> Do you know that if at birth I had been able to make one petition, it would have been that I was born blind? Because when I get to heaven, the first face that shall ever gladden my sight will be that of my Savior.[6]

Fanny Crosby was high-minded. When she sings, "Blessed assurance, Jesus is mine! Oh, what a foretaste of glory divine!" she is proclaiming to the world the beauty of her authentic faith, a gift from God as much as she considered her blindness to be. The gift, the inspiration, the beauty all come from God, even, as Miss Mason says, when those who display it are not religious at all:

> ...every fruitful idea, every original conception, whether in Euclid, or grammar, or music, was a direct inspiration from the Holy Spirit,

without any thought at all as to whether the person so inspired named himself by the name of God, or recognized whence his inspiration came.[7]

This is the stage we set for our study of composers. This is what we must keep in mind, as Miss Mason did—that our sole focus in all education is to gently urge our students toward a life spent glorifying God and basking in His glorious presence. Whenever we can, we should lead our students to dig deeper, to find meaning, to examine the composer's relationship with God and when we see that it was absent, to marvel at His mercy in proffering inspiration anyway.

But what does God want for us? That is the ultimate question, isn't it? We care what Charlotte Mason said about education, but we care more what God has to say to us, personally. Here, I believe again Miss Mason was right to put the receiving of great joy ahead of all else when it came to music appreciation. Suppose God created music and gifted great composers for the sheer pleasure of seeing us experience joy. Could it be that He enjoys seeing our hearts moved and emotions stirred, seeing us dreadfully happy, touched by the same fingertip He used to anoint Bach and Beethoven's work? Certainly there were other reasons for unveiling the gift of music back at the dawn of time, but I'd like to think God also derives pleasure from seeing us moved by it.

Modern society is not terribly concerned with joy. Or beauty. Or anything uplifting and positive. We're seeing world news practically as it happens, and none of it is good. A growing number of us, adults and children alike, are on antidepressant therapy. And yet, look outside your window right now. What do you see? Hopefully a flower. Maybe a blooming rosebush or a plum tree like I do. Is there a butterfly hovering around a milkweed plant? A raindrop resting on a flower petal? Or do you see concrete and hear traffic noise and jets overhead? That's okay, too, because you are resting right where the Father has you.

There is beauty all around us and the possibility of experiencing great joy. But in our quest to fill our minds with tiny packets of news and sayings on social media, we have quickened the pace of thought and neglected to slow down long enough to examine meaning or notice the beauty that is so near. And if we are not noticing what our eyes can see, how will we notice what our ears should hear?

May we slow down long enough to welcome the King of Glory, the Creator of the Universe, with open arms and behold the beauty of His holiness. May we not only see His glory exhibited all around us, but also hear it from the roar of the giant waterfall to the chirping of the newly hatched robin. The God Who decided to give us fragrant plum trees and gardenia bushes, the God Who had the sense of humor to give us giant sunflowers with sturdy stalks and yet has the power to toss lightning bolts across the sky, wants to walk in relationship with us and not only with us but with every human being on the planet, those who know Him and those who don't. He is the same God Who uses broken and fragile vessels to give us music—beautiful music! The God Who chose to bestow the gift of music on genius composers like Mendelssohn, simply for the pleasure of hearing us sing his *Elijah*, is our dear and cherished lover and friend. What a wonder.

This is a selah moment. In fact, we need more selah moments in our days and less busy thinking. The psalmist was right to give us pauses to stop and ponder the meaning of what we have just read or sung. Maybe now would be a good time to stop reading and do a quick search online to find and listen to Chopin's Grand Valse Brillante, Opus 18 in E Flat. I dare you to try not to dance or think of galloping ponies while you listen. After enjoying the cheer Chopin brings, check out the haunting passion of Rimski-Korsakov's Scheherezade. See how the personhood of an individual composer under the inspiration and influence of God can produce vastly different music than another composer equally inspired? Again, what a wonder. Selah.

Are you back? Are you refreshed? Let's move on.

God can use music in innumerable ways to get our attention. It inspires us, heals us, blinds us with its glory, tears at our despairing souls until we choose to seek Him, for nothing else will suffice.

Music can be a loaded weapon. It is filled with the ammunition of power—the power to make a mockery of a political candidate, the power to move a crotchety old man to tears, the power to connect a husband to his wife as she walks down the aisle to be married, the power to move an audience to uproarious laughter, the power to soothe and comfort a rejected and wounded soul, lost and broken. Music packs quite a punch, and it's there waiting for us, to help us manage the tough times and enjoy the blissful seasons, too.

I mentioned Mendelssohn's *Elijah* earlier, and I'd like to share a personal story with you, one that tugs at my heart even today. It's a story about the power of music to touch a human soul. Not only did I sing the *Elijah* back in college at SMU in Dallas (conducted by our wonderful choral director and famed arranger and composer, Lloyd Pfautch), I also remember one song from it for another reason. The piece is "If With All Your Hearts."

My parents divorced when I was thirteen. It was a very messy breakup with lots of heartache and hard feelings on all sides, but primarily on my mother's. My dad left her to marry her best friend, so she lost the two most important emotional connections she had at that time. It happens. I knew that, even as a world-weary young teen. But this time it had happened to me and to *my* family. I was despondent, and so was she. There was no hiding it. We all saw the intense pain in her eyes.

My mother had recently become a born-again Christian, and this memory is indelibly etched in my mind. She was sitting in the dim master bedroom with her autoharp in her arms, strumming quietly and singing mournfully with tears streaming down her cheeks,

If with all your hearts, ye truly seek Me,
Ye shall ever surely find Me.
Thus saith our God.

If you want to know what "with all your hearts" looks like, I submit to you my grieving, heartbroken, tear-stained, devastated mom. What an example of faith amid horrible circumstances she was for the shy, gawky, teenaged me. I'll never forget that song. That moment. The *Elijah*. Or Mendelssohn. Moments of great joy and deep sorrow sting the brain, creating connections that don't disappear over time. This is the power of music to impact a child's life—for good or for ill. May we choose wisely.

We owe a great debt to Felix Mendelssohn, one of the world's greatest composers. We are grateful for his music, for the beauty he left us, and for that great gift from God that sprang from deep within his heart and mind. But I hope each of us also remembers that we leave a legacy of our own to our children, family, friends, and to the world—and that our children are a legacy of sorts as well. What fruit we can help produce within them will continue to bless the world long after we have gone.

Mendelssohn's wife prayed over his coffin after all the mourners had left the church. When someone gently took her arm to lead her away at last, she said, "God will help me, and surely my boys will have the inheritance of some of their father's goodness." Felix Mendelssohn left us his music, but he also left five children to the world—they are his legacy, too. A legacy of goodness. And our children are our legacy, too. I believe that is why we must earnestly pursue what is honorable and good and let nothing supplant it within the hearts of our children. In a way, they are our gift to the world. And beautiful music is a nourishing gift that can aid us in our quest to fill them with what is good and holy and beautiful, but there is music that is not so nourishing, pure, or true. As we steer our children this way and that, it's not always possible to lead them toward still waters and goodness, but I believe our efforts combined with God's love for them will overcome in the end. The music we place before them, beginning at an early age, will take root in their hearts and nourish them for later work. And it may be that your child will become the world's next brilliant composer, the world's next Mendelssohn, Brahms, or Chopin. Time will tell. A broad feast awaits.

Miss Mason assures us that parents are the prime suppliers of a child's mind nourishment, especially in the early years. As she says, " ... a woman may in her heedlessness let fly upon her offspring a thousand ills. But is there not also 'a glass of blessings standing by,' into which parents may dip, and bring forth for their children health and vigour, justice and mercy, truth and beauty?"[8]

The beauty of opening a lifelong love of music—good, quality, earnest, well-written music composed by the great masters of the craft, contributes much to the glass of blessings. Let us drink deeply and share generously.

There is nothing in the world so much like prayer as music is.
— *William P. Merrill*

Chapter Two

Becoming a Listener:
The Power of Enthusiasm and
the Joy of Steady Effort

Not only our little nameless acts, but the great purposes of our lives, arise out of our feelings. Enthusiasm itself is not thought, though it arises when we are 'stung with the rapture of a sudden thought'; it is a glowing, malleable condition of the forces of our nature, during which all things are possible to us, and we only wait for a lead.[9]

—*Charlotte Mason, Parents and Children*

nthusiasm is not in our everyday vocabulary as teachers. We don't say to our children, "Muster up some enthusiasm for English grammar and math, please!" We also do not tend to think of it as something we must pretend to have, merely for the sake of our children "catching the vision" and learning to love a subject. That would be false and stilted and wrong. Plus, most children are intelligent and intuitive enough to see right through our false faces.

So we have a potential problem raising delighted listeners. A child will soak up ideas, thoughts, knowledge, and habits from his parents. If a mother and father are not enthusiastic about music study or music appreciation, there is a strong likelihood that the children under their care will not be particularly interested in them either. But we are busy home educators, teachers, and parents with multiple plates spinning in the air. The idea of becoming enthusiastic supporters of symphonic music, for parents who were not raised on a daily diet of it to begin with, is daunting. What is to be done?

I think we need to become learners alongside our children. If you have never heard a particular piece before or have never heard of a certain composer, it's more than acceptable to learn as you go, right along with your student(s). Hopefully, you will have set the stage for them to become strong in the habit of attention prior to beginning composer study, so there they may have the advantage. But give yourself time and space to grow and learn. (For those of you who are new to a Charlotte Mason education, the habit of attention is an important component during the early years and builds a foundation for steady attention in all areas of life later on.)

America's first female violin virtuoso, Maud Powell, urged young violinists to bask in their early enthusiasm for music, and I think we would do well to listen to her advice, even if we are not instrumentalists but listeners:

> Remember the impression of that first bloom of enthusiasm, that first warm appeal. You will lose it all presently, when your soul flounders in a cloud of technical drudgery. The fresh enthusiasm will be deadened during the process of memorizing, while difficult passage work is practiced in sections, and countless repetition stretches patience to its limit. Some day when the composition is conquered and is yours, the warm glow of enthusiasm will return.[10]

Our children need to see our effort and our enthusiasm, to see us extend our energy toward music appreciation. In fact, that may be all they need to see at first. We don't have to go overboard and pile on the picture book biographies, music lessons, and classical music in the car, as background music during school, and piped outside during free play and nature study. We could do that, but for the very young child it's not necessary. I think it's worth mentioning that beginning instrument lessons too early can be detrimental, too. We need to first become good listeners. In *The Term's Music*, Glover reminds us:

> It is obviously an advantage for a child who is temperamentally so inclined, to learn to play an instrument and to interpret music for

himself, but too much time is often spent in turning a potentially good listener into an indifferent executant, and incidentally stifling the spark of enthusiasm by hopeless and unrewarded drudgery.[11]

The importance of enthusiasm cannot be stressed enough. Children become curious when they see their parents enjoying something—a special coffee drink, for example, that once in a great while they may be allowed a sip of, just the tiniest taste. What joy! What a privilege for a four-year-old! So it can be with music appreciation. Let them see you tear up over a Puccini aria. Act out the Anvil Chorus from Il Trovatore with them, slinging an imaginary hammer as you listen. These are the moments that make composer study a lively, exciting event rather than a silent (dull) listening time, while drinking tea solemnly at the dining room table using music as the background for learning table manners.

WHAT QUALIFIES US AS LISTENERS?

Absolutely nothing is required of you to become a listener. We would never suggest that only those with musical talent should have the good fortune of listening to music. That would make it solely the pleasure of the elite, the instrumentalists or singers who prove that they can perform. This is the opposite of what Miss Mason claimed, that all deserve a rich, liberal feast of living ideas, a wide table spread with all types of knowledge, not the least of which (I promise!) is musical knowledge. Glover says, "To limit the study of music to the so-called 'musical' is just as reasonable as to close the theatres to all who have no talent for acting, or to forbid the picture galleries to all who cannot paint."[12]

WHEN DO WE BEGIN?

According to Mrs. Curwen, a contemporary of Miss Mason's who was an important figure in her views on music study, "Music teaching begins in the nursery, in the cradle. For from the time the baby's 'five gateways of knowledge' begin to open and admit sense impressions, the little ears should be often greeted by sweet musical sounds. And we do sing to our babies. It is one of the wonderful results of motherhood that the woman who never sang before will find herself singing to her little baby."[13]

Singing to babies is a far cry from actual instrument lessons or sight-reading, of course. During the early years, enjoying music is of the utmost importance. We can trust in Glover's advice and refuse to stifle our children's enthusiasm for music by forcing them at increasingly earlier ages to learn an instrument. Preschoolers are far too busy taking in knowledge, and attention spans at such an early age are short.

Miss Mason said we must allow the children time to grow into a deep appreciation of music before they begin actual instrumental training, and I agree. But neither of us gets the final word when it comes to your child. The only possible exception to this standard that I can see is Suzuki violin training. A child of three years old can begin learning the basics, and becoming a part of a larger group of musical sojourners can be deeply rewarding. Should we or shouldn't we? I'll defer here to the individual family, who, after much prayer and fully understanding the needs of each particular child, may choose to enroll their student in early instrument training. Mrs. Curwen says in rare cases it is allowable, and it is up to each of us to decide if our child is that prodigy or has the maturity and ability to undertake early lessons. Freedom in Christ is key here.

Nothing within these pages ought to be seen as a restraint or cause you to hold back in any way if the Lord is urging you forward. We live in a different era than Miss Mason did, and there are going to be distinctions that pertain to our society—situations she never faced, pressures she did not have to deal with, research she wasn't privy to. I suggest you bring all things before God in prayer and move forward from there.

WHERE DO WE BEGIN?

Miss Mason, in her PNEU Programmes, shows us that a full and nourishing music education requires more than merely choosing a composer and listening to six pieces per term. Surprised? I was, too. Miss Mason believed the first step toward developing a love of music lies in cultivating a strong ear for the ordinary tones and melodies found all around us. Nature is our best and first teacher for this, from our children's earliest years. As we go about our daily lives, spending time with our children outdoors in quiet, undisturbed observation as well as boisterous play, we can help them become good listeners. There are countless sounds to be enjoyed, from the buzzing of the cicada to the cooing of the mourning dove, if only we take the time to notice them.

In *Parents and Children*, Miss Mason urges this type of noticing:

A quick and true ear is another possession that does not come by nature, or anyway, if it does, it is too often lost. How many sounds can you distinguish in a sudden silence out of doors? Let these be named in order from the less to the more acute. Let the notes of the birds be distinguished, both call-notes and song-notes; the four or five distinct sounds to be heard in the flow of a brook. Cultivate accuracy in distinguishing footfalls and voices; in discerning, with their eyes shut, the direction from which a sound proceeds, in which footsteps are moving. Distinguish passing vehicles by the sounds; as lorry, brougham, dog-cart. Music is, no doubt, the means *par excellence* for this kind of ear culture.[14]

She reiterates this same notion again, later, in *Ourselves*, and the passage is so lovely that I've copied it in its entirety below. As you read, picture the area surrounding your home or perhaps a local nature preserve or nearby park, someplace your family might make frequent visits to and form relationships with the plants, flowers, birds, and animals. Could this be your listening space?

Have you ever been in the fields on a spring day, and heard nothing at all but your own voice and the voices of your companions, and then, perhaps, suddenly you have become silent, and you find a concert going on of which you had not heard a note? At first you hear the voices of the birds; then, by degrees, you perceive high voices, low voices, and middle voices, small notes and great notes, and you begin to wish you knew who sang each of the songs you can distinguish.

Then, as you listen more, you hear more. The chirp of the

grasshoppers becomes so noisy that you wonder you can hear yourself speak for it; then the bees have it all to themselves in your hearing; then you hear the hum or the trumpet of smaller insects, and perhaps the tinkle and gurgle of a stream. The quiet place is full of many sounds, and you ask yourself how you could have been there without hearing them. That just shows you how Hearing may sleep at his post. Keep him awake and alive; make him try to hear and know some new sound every day without any help from sight. It is rather a good plan to listen with shut eyes.

Have you ever heard the beech-leaves fall one by one in the autumn? That is a very nice sound. Have you heard the tap, tap of the woodpecker, or have you heard a thrush breaking snail-shells on a stone? ... Do you listen to people's voices, and can you tell by the intonation whether the people are sad or glad, pleased or displeased?[15]

I tried this with my grandchildren recently and was forced to face a certain uncomfortable reality. I have allowed too much worry and anxiety to invade my inward thoughts. The moment I told the children, ages 5, 3, and 2, to stop chattering and listen for nature sounds, they heard things I did not— and they stopped their playing repeatedly throughout the next hour to tell me there was yet another new bird nearby and that the squirrel they had heard earlier was farther away now. How extraordinary that they took to this new adventure in listening so quickly! I was quite surprised at how good they were at it, and a little ashamed at my own rusty listening skills. Hopefully, in time I will improve!

As I was pondering this idea of learning to really listen to the world around me as a precursor to listening intently to classical music, I began digging a bit more. I found some interesting ideas on place, on sound, on the beauty of experiencing the world through sound as opposed to how we generally tend to view it—with our eyes. Even using the word "view" lends to sight rather than sound, but seeing is only one of our senses. Is listening not at least equally important?

In my eagerness to better understand this concept, I came upon an interview with Acoustic Ecologist (yes, there is such a thing) Gordon Hempton in which he described a day of professional listening at Olympic National Park in Seattle, Washington. Hempton has opened my eyes to an entirely new way of thinking about sound. I almost wish you could read this next portion with your eyes closed, but that would be rather difficult! Try to imagine, if you will, the stillness and quiet of a meadow or forest. You are all alone, and no one will interrupt you with words. This may be tough, considering there is almost always a child in need of a restroom break or a skinned knee to soothe whenever we are out with young children. But Hempton's point is that we need to try to develop this new way of "looking" at the world through our ears:

No more than 100 yards along the tall, tree-lined, ferned path with moss drapes that add sound-deadening to the experience, we'll hear the far-off twitter of a Winter Wren, this very high-pitched twittering sound that might be coming from 100 feet away.

And then we'll hear further away the sound of the Hoh River that drains the Rain Forest echoing off the far side of the valley. And if we were taking this hike in the fall, we would hear the bugling of the Roosevelt elk. Up close, it's actually quite a guttural, adrenalin-filled assertion of what it means to be male and wild.

When you're in a quiet place, your listening horizon extends for miles in every direction. When you hear an elk call from miles away, it turns into a magic flute as the result of traveling through this place that has the same acoustics as a cathedral. I hear the presence of everything.[16]

Hearing the presence of everything is a tall order and a gift that will take time to cultivate, but do try! Practicing attentive listening is a skill Miss Mason has challenged us to develop and one that will serve us well in the future.

Mrs. Curwen once said, "Many play the piano well, but never listen at all, because music is taught through the eye and not through the ear, which is almost as foolish as trying to teach drawing by smell."[17] She goes on to say, "... the longer I live, the more convinced I am that in music teaching the key to the whole situation is ear-training, ear-training, ear-training." Just as we begin with the habit of attention in young children, so we should begin training them to listen from an early age.

Judging by the enjoyment Gordon Hempton has found sitting in nature and simply listening, I think we can safely trust in Miss Mason's ideas here. A child needs to explore his world during the preschool years, and part of that exploration should include the sense of hearing, probably more than it generally does in our modern culture.

Once these early years of dawdling days spent listening to nature's gripping melodies give way to a more disciplined type of study, Mrs. Curwen's Teacher's Guide to The Child Pianist has quite a lot to tell us about the natural process of learning about music. Here we have Miss Mason's full endorsement:

Mrs.Curwen's 'Child Pianist' puts carefully graduated work of this kind into the hands of parents; and, if a child never becomes a performer, to have acquired a cultivated and correct ear is no small part of a musical education.[18]

We will consider Mrs. Curwen's recommendations in detail in a later chapter, but here is her basic outline for the early years. Surrounding your children with music from birth to age 4-5 by singing to them while rocking them is the first step in a child's music education. It allows the very young child to associate music with the comfort, pleasure and sweetness of resting in safety in Mom or Dad's lap:

> The musical nurse, who croons old ditties while rocking the children to sleep, or dandles them on her knee to the well-marked rhythm of a country dance, is a powerful factor in their musical development, and such music lessons should be made a part of nursery training long before schoolroom or governess is dreamt of.[19]

Our children did not have a nurse to sing them "ditties," but every night they listened to a cassette tape we picked up at (of all places) Victoria's Secret, the lingerie store. This was the last thing they heard before falling asleep each night. It was a composite of several soft classics from Beethoven to Chopin. Even now, whenever my children hear one of those pieces, their hearts are filled with joy. They can't possibly remember why, but we know it was that early, soft, lilting music that associated peace and calm with melody and harmony. Just last week, I heard a Borodin piece on the radio, and it took me right back to that cassette tape.

This sort of repeated listening will eventually enable your children or students to recognize the work of various composers. Style and technique are often absorbed without the child realizing it. Miss Mason said in *Ourselves*:

> Many great men have put their beautiful thoughts, not into books, or
> pictures, or buildings, but into musical score, to be sung with the voice
> or played on instruments, and so full are these musical compositions of
> the minds of their makers, that people who care for music can always
> tell who has composed the music they hear, even if they have never
> heard the particular movement before. ... Quite little children can
> sometimes get a good deal of this power; indeed, I knew a boy of
> three years old who knew when his mother was playing 'Wagner,' for
> example. She played to him a great deal, and he listened.[20]

When Mrs Curwen referred to music education in her *Parents' Review*
article, "Music Teaching," she emphasized the importance of taking stock of
the child's existing store of ideas about music. She believed children need an
early music vocabulary, just the basics, so that when they are ready to begin
instrument training they will have something on which to hang the new
knowledge they will be attaining. This makes sense to me. As we transition
from listening intently to nature sounds to singing nursery songs with nanny
(or mom or caregiver or teacher), each day will bring fresh knowledge about
music—today perhaps we'll learn what a staff is and tomorrow what a quarter
note rest looks like. Maybe we will practice drawing three perfect rests or do
some clapping rhythms along with a folk song.

Mrs. Curwen said, "The first step of the pianoforte teacher, as of any
other teacher, should be to correct whatever ideas may be wrong; to clear up
those that are hazy and to fill up gaps; and then to make that existing store
of knowledge the starting-point for her own instruction."[21] This tells me that
we need to offer our children an "apperception mass" to use a Herbartian
phrase—a cluster of stored knowledge about the topic of music—from an early
age so that they will have some basic understanding of its form and function
before official music lessons begin.

These are fun years. Nursery songs, dances, chants, and clapping games
take center stage when children are young and carefree, spending afternoons
outdoors in the sunshine. Once official teaching begins at around age six, and
this would only be singing classes or folk song and hymn time, you can assess

each child's attainments. Mrs. Curwen said:

> The ideas he has been storing up through all the early years can be,
> as it were, brought out and examined and compared, and judgments
> formed about them. The concrete wholes, which the child calls tunes,
> can be broken up into their elements of pitch and rhythm and you will
> readily see that the larger the child's experience, the more material he
> has with which to experiment, the more likely he is to discover those
> simple natural laws which, when classified and labeled, we call musical
> theory. All this, if it is done at all, must be done by ear training. It is
> to the ear that every new effect of pitch or rhythm must be presented,
> and the ear should be satisfied that a thing is so before that thing is
> symbolized by a note or labeled with a name. It is the ear that must
> examine, compare, and judge, and recollect.[22]

Mrs. Curwen mentioned that children need to strengthen their fingers
and wrists for future instrument playing. She even referenced certain exercises
that might be performed during kindergarten drill. I was not able to find
the exercises she spoke of, but I imagine spending some family time doing
handicrafts like simple knitting with large needles, weaving, crocheting, drawing
and tracing, painting, coloring within the lines, etc., would all prepare small
fingers for later piano playing. I did find some interesting gadgets online that
claim to strengthen finger dexterity. These hand strengtheners are around $25
each. I don't know any preschooler who would want to sit quietly exercising his
or her fingers with one of them, but you never know.

The most important thing to remember in the early years is that a love
for classical music is caught, not taught. Enjoy music in front of your young
children. Sing to them, with them, and don't ever stop. A final caveat from
Mrs. Curwen:

> We are told that baby is to be taught to observe, and so we are always
> saying, "Look, Baby, look." Might we not a little oftener say, "Listen,
> Baby, listen?" We sing to the little ones to achieve a present purpose—
> to send them to sleep, and when they can get to sleep without the song
> we leave off singing. But if we realized that by going on we are laying

in a stock of material for future use, we would attend to nursery music as religiously as to nursery diet and hygiene.[23]

   This is an important concept: we are laying in a stock of material for future use. Every nursery song, jingle, rhyme, clapping game, and hymn or prayer you teach your young children will add to the stored material they have to pull from in later years. We don't need to start with Mozart, Bach, or Brahms. We can begin with Mary Had a Little Lamb and Jesus Loves Me. We are building a library in the House of Mind. It hasn't many shelves yet, nor loads of books and great thoughts of the Masters, but in time the fullness will arrive and bring with it a wealth of relationships, deep and wide.

...The instrument, whether it be a piano or a violin or a voice, is only a medium for that strange and impalpable something which to the majority of mankind seems as necessary as the breath of Heaven.

                                                    —Annie Jessy Curwen

Chapter Three

Form and Instrumentation:
The Bricks and Mortar of Genius

Oh, the misery of having something of infinite, though perhaps esoteric, beauty fall on ears that do not understand! Little do people realize what joys lie in store for them if they would seek and humbly prepare their minds with a little study.

—*Maud Powell, "The American Girl and Her Violin"*

As a child grows older, there are other ways to cultivate a strong ear for music. According to Percy Scholes, author of *The Listener's Guide to Music*, a child should learn a bit about orchestral instruments, the basics of form, and about the composer's time, culture, and background. Marjorie Ransom reiterates these ideas in her *Parents' Review* article, "Art and Literature in the Parents' Union School":

> About six works by some great composer are chosen for study each term. These compositions are played or sung to the children constantly and *studied carefully*. [italics mine] The children are taught something about the form, harmonic structure, thematic development of the composition and some information is given about the life of the composer. An article appears every term in the *Parents' Review* on the composer and his works, which is a great help to the teacher or parent

who is giving the musical appreciation lessons.[24]

We who have studied and implemented Miss Mason's methods quote this article often in an effort to steer new teachers toward studying six works by a great composer each term. But rarely do we address the other suggestions within the article—studying form, harmonic structure, and thematic development. There is more to the subject of composer study than we previously thought! Sadly, we have not quite understood all that Miss Mason intended for her students when it came to appreciating music. Only recently, with the availability of public domain books online, have we been able to access the books Miss Mason used, so we can hardly be blamed for the oversight. But is there a remedy for our negligence? And is a deeper study of music and composers even necessary in the twenty-first century? I believe it is. And yes, there is a remedy.

Here, we again turn to Glover. In *The Term's Music*, he explains that the broader musical knowledge a child gains from learning how music works and improving his or her own musical skill is important:

The very science and system of music constitutes its first charm; we will find the history of the science little by little unfolds what makes it most romantic and at last the dullest of picturesque, five-finger exercises and most tiresome of scales will become invested with a sort of glamour or poetry which will be welcomed by the student who is really zealous as part of what one day will be the real glory of a great achievement.[25]

We don't often think of repeated scales and music practice as glamorous or poetic, do we? Yet, there is a certain amount of ordinary grunt work associated with achievement. We cannot reach for perfection in music performance without practicing a piece until it becomes our own and then practicing it some more to reach a level where we can focus on the dynamics—this part needs to be louder, then soft again here with a staccato note at the end of the phrase, etc. Learning a difficult piece of music takes hard, steady effort, and in order to produce a work of great beauty, we must be willing to work sacrificially to achieve it.

The key here is finding the glory of God within the practice or work and not only in the final product. Glover says we should celebrate the science and system of music itself, which allows us to replicate the piece created by a great master with our own hands. This is true "musical appreciation." Once we have performed it ourselves, we really do appreciate it all the more. (And for those of us who never managed to squeak past the intermediate performance level, it also develops a fresh perspective on the genius of composing.)

Mrs. Davenport, in her *Parents' Review* article "Of Piano Playing," had this to say:

Technique and expression are almost too nearly allied for a child to distinguish between them. If the melody is singing sweetly, clearly, and sustainedly in one hand, and the other is accompanying firmly, quietly, and in perfect time, let that be enough. In the after years when life has opened out in all directions, and the mind is full of the mystery of human life, and the heart is full of love, and maybe sorrow, then expression will come. But first must come a love of every detail of the learning; an unwearying devotion; and an honest determination to spare no trouble in the attaining. Did not a great man [Thomas Carlyle] once say that even genius was only 'an infinite capacity for taking pains?'[26]

Every great composer has had to learn the theory of music, has had to learn about each instrument and what it does to serve the orchestra. Understanding design in music is paramount to creating it. The master of design, with inspiration from the greatest Master of all, can create sustained beauty in music. It is a joint effort, and there is a tension to the relationship. A composer cannot create inspired music without the Inspirer Himself. But God does not simply download music, fully formed, into the waiting composer's head as if he or she is a computer awaiting holy software. God anoints the hard effort of the composer. He enables, imparts, and imbues us with everything we need to produce a masterpiece. Scholes, in his *Listener's Guide to Music*, worries that people may look on the composer as "a mere channel or lightning conductor which collects the electric fluid from the heavens and conveys it to the hearts of men." It's true. When we think of inspiration, we don't often consider the years of steady effort it took for the composer to learn and hone his craft, years spent in toil late at night, perhaps in a highly caffeinated state, learning the art of composition. Scholes says of those who misunderstand how inspiration works:

> If these people were to put on paper their picture of a composer at work it would be something like this: a wild-eyed creature, with ruffled hair, seated at an untidy table with music-paper before him, and writing, writing, writing, feverishly and excitedly the thoughts that Heaven sends. 'Inspiration' is percolating from the ether into his brain, in burning streams it flows down his arm, into his hand, out at his fingertips and along his pen, from which it drips over the paper in black-headed crotchets and quavers. The creature rises with a shout of joy. A masterpiece is born![27]

Scholes reminds us that symphonies do not come into the world that way. Inspiration and design work hand in hand. He says that of all pieces of art that fail, some fail for lack of inspiration, some for lack of good design, and others for some problem with the execution. We would find it odd to think of a poet or author's eyes rolling back in their heads as they hear from the spirits what to write and jot it down, yet we believe that is how composers write music. Not so.

Edgar Allan Poe wrote an essay titled "The Philosophy of Composition," in which he suggests most writers are happy for their readers to believe divine inspiration came upon them in an ecstatic burst as they wrote the book. A peek behind the curtain, so to speak, reveals a distinctly different truth, and it's not quite as pretty. He says the public would see, "the elaborate and vacillating crudities of thought ... innumerable glimpses of idea ... discarded in despair as unmanageable ... selections and rejections ... painful erasures and interpolations."[28] In other words, writing is not easy. As Thomas Edison said of inventing, it's "one percent inspiration and ninety-nine percent perspiration."

Beethoven was well aware of what Poe calls "painful erasures." When he died, he left behind more than fifty sketchbooks filled with notes and notation. Whenever he had the germ of an idea, he quickly jotted it down in a notebook he kept with him at all times—in his pocket or beside his bed. Beethoven was a notebook keeper, just like a Charlotte Mason student, only his commonplace books were filled with music. Mendelssohn once followed a passage written by Beethoven from its beginning to its final form. He found it had changed thirteen times and that the thirteenth version was exactly the same as the original one. That sounds quite a lot like the ninety-nine percent Edison was talking about.

Bach spent long hours copying out the works of the great Italian and French composers who came before him. Handel traveled Europe listening to different symphonies in different countries to get ideas. Elgar studied Beethoven's first symphony in detail to learn how he managed to get certain effects across in the music. Mozart was constantly lost in thought. He worked out design primarily within his mind rather than on paper, but he was nonetheless carefully planning and executing design in his works, whether at the dinner table while grasping his napkin or tapping his feet as he washed his face at the washbasin in the morning. Design in music takes steady effort. It is definitely not for the weak of heart.

Music is human expression in sound, but according to rules and principles. Does the young listener need to know the rules in order to enjoy the music? To a certain extent, no. But if Tolstoy had been given just a few lessons, he might never have written this:

> An acquaintance of yours, a musician of repute, sits down to the piano and plays you what he says is a new composition ... You hear the strange, loud sounds and admire the gymnastic exercises performed by his fingers; and you see that the performer wishes to impress on you that the sounds he is producing express various poetic strivings of the soul. You see his intention, but no feeling whatever is transmitted to you except weariness....[29]

Alas! Poor Tolstoy! It has been said that he could understand a simple folk song but not a symphony. Scholes agreed: "Tolstoy would abolish all complex music because the plain man cannot grasp it at a sitting. The assumption of the present book is that it is better to abolish the plain man as a plain man. There is a world of beauty lying just beyond that plain man's reach; it is worth a little striving on his part to find the way to that world and enter in."[30]

Children who study a bit of notation, composition, and music theory will appreciate a composer even more than those who have no knowledge of it whatsoever. They may even catch a glimpse of his patterns and designs and structures as they listen. And they may create great musical compositions of their own one day. In order to offer a wide feast and to open as many avenues of relationship as we possibly can, we need to be aware that our children or students may one day fulfill their callings as artists or musicians. It is not outside the realm of possibility. We teach math as if they may one day want to become engineers; we teach science as if we believe they may grow up to find a cure for cancer. We should take artistic endeavors at least as seriously.

LEARNING ABOUT INSTRUMENTATION

Scholes explains that learning about instruments can enrich a child's understanding of music. Many adults of a certain age grew up listening to Benjamin Britten's "Young Person's Guide to the Orchestra" or Mitch Miller's "A Child's Introduction to the Orchestra and All Its instruments."[31] Works like these will both help students identify the individual instruments they are hearing in orchestral music, which will, in turn, aid them in their overall appreciation of music.

Miss Mason believed children should attend live performances so that they might experience music firsthand rather than from a recording. While this isn't always possible, it does much to help them identify the instruments. We can also give our students firsthand experience with orchestral instruments by taking them to the symphony, arriving early, and walking them up to the stage to watch the musicians warm up. As the daughter of symphony musicians, I can assure you that they do not mind children watching, even up close. As professionals, they have performed these pieces multiple times and each performance, while special to the audience, can become tedious and monotonous to the musicians. Knowing that a child is interested in learning about his instrument could brighten the evening for a performer who is playing Beethoven's Fifth for the thousandth time.

Some orchestras have a "petting zoo" where children can hold and play the different instruments. These experiences are generally offered before a children's concert. Attending a musical petting zoo can inspire a child to take lessons and learn to play an instrument. Many a young violinist began this way, although I can't vouch for tuba players or percussionists.

Attending a live performance can go a long way toward building a child's relationship with the music. As Scholes says: "He notes a little theme taken up in turn by the clear-voiced flute, the rich-toned clarinet, and the thin-sounding, piquant oboe. He marvels at the variety of effects of the great body of fiddles, little and big, playing softly or loudly, bowing or plucking their strings, muted or unmuted, he admires the warm tone of the horns playing slow chords. The colouring of the piece is now clear to him."[32]

I have gathered some listening recommendations from professional musicians that feature individual orchestral instruments. I asked not only music professors, teachers, and conductors but, specifically, orchestral musicians who actually play the instruments for which they are recommending pieces. The list quickly became unwieldy, which is a good thing. I had too many recommendations to include in a single chapter, so I've added it as Appendix G. Don't forget to flip to the back of the book and find it. There are so many gems there. At some point, grab a cup of tea and your computer and find the links to these pieces. You will quickly learn to pick out the different instruments in the orchestra while listening.

LEARNING THE BASICS OF FORM

Music can be subdivided much the same way a story can—into musical sentences, paragraphs, and phrases that, together, make a whole movement or piece. Likewise, each piece follows a certain format, much the same way an essay follows a format: persuasive, expository, narrative. We don't speak "music;" we speak English. So there is often a large learning curve when it comes to understanding musical form. Taking a slow, steady look at form, beginning with the first composer you study, won't take long, propped up by our friend the internet search engine. Here we can learn about Bach's cantatas, Beethoven's symphonies, Handel's oratorios, Mozart's requiem, and Chopin's impromptus, perhaps adding to our "form" vocabulary with one new word per composer. Did the composer write this piece in sonata form? Is it a rondo? Take some time to familiarize yourself with the basics of form and incorporate these new words into your music vocabulary.

There are different names for different types of musical stories. A requiem is written for a funeral or to commemorate a death. A minuet is dance music.

The word symphony comes from the Greek symphonia, which means harmony. It is derived from syn, which means together, and phone, which means voice or sound. A symphony, then, is simply sounds being played together. A symphony will always have three or four movements or sections, and some even have five. Each one will be different from the previous one. The first movement might be fast, while the second is slower. The third movement might be a dance. This is all part of the overall form of the piece.

In *The Story of Music and Musicians for Young Readers*, Lucy Lillie tells us that the history of an opera or an oratorio is as charming as any fairy tale and that the science in it "has its picturesque side." She tells us that following the study of music with a "conscientious regard for its higher meanings and its original starting points" is never dull work.[33] If we approach the study of form as we do any other study—using Miss Mason's methods to enliven it and enlarge it, even the more mundane bits can appear miraculous. Who gifted the composer with the ability to order music into phrases, structures, and wholes? The answer is the same God Whose Mathematics were used to form the universe. The same God Who created the math of the ever-expanding universe is present to anoint and advise and touch the heart of the composer, even to the point of revealing the magnificent intricacies of the rondo or the masterful extravagance of the oratorio. When we read that it took Handel only three weeks to write *The Messiah* and approximately three days to write the Hallelujah Chorus, we marvel. "The kingdom of our Lord and of His Christ" are present, even within the form and format of a piece of music, and that recognition alone is awe-inspiring. Finding the miraculous within the form is not only possible but essential to igniting a passion for musical knowledge within your children or students.

I do want to mention one more thing. Within the books Miss Mason used, the word form was often categorized to mean something closer to "format." A symphony, a motet, a concerto—these are formats a composer might choose. Today, most of us understand form in music to mean how the piece is organized rather than what its format is. Sonata form is generally ABA. Merriam-Webster defines it as "a musical form that consists basically of an exposition, a development, and a recapitulation, that is used especially for the first movement of a sonata." So we have sonata form (a melody, further development of the melody, and back to the original melody) and the sonata itself (the name of a piece that was written using sonata form). Confused? Well, it is a little confusing. Here is another example. Twinkle, Twinkle, Little Star is a children's nursery song (format) written in Ternary Form, which is similar to Sonata Form in that it is organized into three parts: ABA.

Part A: Twinkle, twinkle, little star, how I wonder what you are.
Part B: Up above the world so high, like a diamond in the sky.
Part A (again): Twinkle, twinkle, little star, how I wonder what you are.

For now, let's remember that a little research goes a long way. You don't need to know a rhapsody from an etude or a fugue from a sonata—not at first, anyway. These terms will become a part of your lives soon enough. With each composer you study, you'll gain a bit more confidence and learn better how to identify the style, tone, and type of piece you're listening to. But by no means is this the ultimate goal of listening. Enjoying the music, becoming enveloped in its glory, experiencing the joy it brings, recognizing that God has gifted a human vessel to write such a piece—these are what is truly needful. The rest will come in due time.

LEARNING ABOUT A COMPOSER'S LIFE

After all this talk of the theoretical, it is easy to get bogged down and wonder if we will even find the time to lay down these additional avenues in the House of Mind. It was hard enough to fit listening time into our already jam-packed school days. But I believe Miss Mason had a reason for everything she required of children, and this attention to form and instrumentation in music is no exception. However, it is even more important to help children form lasting connections with composers. Scholes in his *Listener's Guide* and Miss Mason in her volumes both stress the importance of relationship. Once our children reach elementary school age and definitely when they reach the sometimes turbulent and emotional middle school years, they need to feel connected to the composer in some way. They must feel he's a dear and trusted friend. Scholes says that when a child has built a relationship with a composer by learning about that composer's life, "the piece is no longer a tour de force of technical achievement, but … a medium of human expression."[34] Relationship is key within a Charlotte Mason education, and a warm relationship or friendship with a composer can bring a child endless joy.

We will devote a substantial amount of time to this friendship in later chapters, not only because I believe it is the single most important facet of music appreciation but also because when we read about these master musicians of old, we can see once again the sacred thread that weaves itself throughout history—the idea that God has anointed men and women with genius and presented them to us for His good pleasure and our great joy. They are our genius mentors, but they are also our dear, beloved friends.

Music is a friend of labor for it lightens the task by refreshing the nerves and spirit of the worker.

—William Green

Chapter Four

Minds Revitalized:
Knowledge Acquired through Story

All deep things are song. It seems somehow the very central essence of us, song;
as if all the rest were but wrappages and hulls!

—*Thomas Carlyle*

A ccording to Miss Mason, a generous curriculum always includes stories: fairy tales, heroic journeys, biographies, histories—stories that inspire us to live better, to be better human beings. Miss Mason believed a well-told tale could breathe the Holy Spirit's urge toward right living directly into the soul of a child, effortlessly and without parental or teacher intervention. And what joy there is to be found between the covers of a well-crafted work of fiction.

We read living books because they are engaging and filled with beauty, yet they also serve another purpose. What is read in literary form is more easily retained than non-fiction accounts that are overladen with dry facts. We need story, then, because it helps us remember what we have read. We read Marshall's *Our Island Story* to learn about the history of England, and there are others: *A Child's History of the World* by Hillyer, *50 Famous Stories Retold* by Baldwin, Van Loon's *Story of Mankind*, Bachman's *The Story of Inventions*.

When studying the lives of great composers, we want to know their stories, too. It helps us relate to them as human beings, but it also invigorates the study of music to learn even a few tidbits about each composer—some items of note that will help us differentiate one from another or some interesting and lively ideas they had about music and life. Sometimes their stories will be inspiring, especially if they were devoted to serving God and mankind. Other times their lives were scandalous, but every event, every life decision they made led to the making of glorious music as an extension of their personhood. Some stories are tragic, like that of our dear Schubert, whose life was cut short by syphilis. Others were victorious, like those of Bach or Handel.

But I need to mention something else here before we dive into story. Miss Mason put her trust in the books of Hubert Parry, Percy Scholes, and a few other carefully selected authors. I decided to read these books and find out what made them so special to a discerning educator like Miss Mason. I was enchanted by their readability but also astonished at the way they looked at music and its creators as a whole, rather than separating the composition from the composer or the instrument from the composition. She chose books that covered every aspect of music, weaving the stories of the composers into the study of form, history, literature (even Shakespeare), genre, and technique. What a fantastic idea! You can see this weaving of history, geography, form, instrumentation, and story in the table of contents from Scholes' *The First Book of the Great Musicians:*

English Music in the Days of Drake and Shakespeare
Henry Purcell: The Greatest British Composer
C-O-N-T-R-A-P-U-N-T-A-L: A Big Word Explained
All about Fugues and How to Listen to Them
Haydn
Mozart
Sonatas and Symphonies
Beethoven
What is an Orchestra
Schumann
Chopin
What is Romantic Music?
Grieg and his Norwegian Music

Scholes did not simply write a book about the lives of the composers, filled with biographical information to supplement our listening time (six pieces by each composer per term). His book was more than likely chosen because the feast must be laid out as a banquet of living ideas, not tidy packages that fit nicely into the organized rows or ruts that we have created for our children. We have to be careful to lay out the proper nourishment, but not to the point of placing it within rigid structures that can quite easily become strangleholds.

I'm excited to share these new revelations with you so that you, too, can reap the rewards of this alteration in method. I believe it works particularly well when studying a subject that requires skill as well as knowledge. We can learn much about history, for example, from a living book, but there is no special key to learning how history works—not in the same sense as algebraic equations or chemical compounds. In other words, we learn about history, but we do not learn how to do history. Does that make sense? We may note a few trends here and there or analyze military movements and overarching themes, but these are all learned through reading and understanding the unfolding of the story.

Literature exists for us to read and enjoy the intricacies of the plot, but writing itself is a skill. We generally study them separately, but it's also possible to join the two and use living books to teach the skill of writing. See the difference? Learning to understand the form, instrumentation, and composition of music and learning to play an instrument or read music is a skill, just as writing is a skill. Including technique, form, and instrumentation within the pages of a living book on music and its composers is an ingenius way to help students absorb the skills they will need to one day be musicians themselves. Again, we see Miss Mason's mind at work in her book recommendations. And we see, too, that not just any biography will do.

I'd like to give you a little foretaste of what delectable ideas you'll find in these books and what relationships students will form with music and its makers. Here's a snapshot from Chapter 2 of Percy Scholes' *The First Book of the Great Musicians*. Notice how he weaves history in with hymns and psalms, story, and form. This is a public domain book, so I am offering you a large excerpt here. I think it's important to see and understand the type of living music book Miss Mason wanted us to read. (Apologies in advance for the offensive misuse of the word "savages.")

When Francis Drake set out on his expedition round the world in 1577, tiny though his ship was, he yet found room in it for musicians. You would imagine that he would use all his little space for sailors and soldiers; but it was not so, and at meal-times he always had the musicians play before him. A Spanish admiral whom he took prisoner and whose diary has lately been printed says 'the Dragon' (for that was what the Spaniards called Drake) 'always dined and supped to the music of viols'. ...

Drake's crew were great singers, and when they went on shore in another place, and built a fort to stay in for a time, the savages used to come to hear them sing their psalms and hymns at the time of prayers. ...

If you read the chaplain's book, *The World Encompassed*, you will find many other little stories that will show you how musical were Drake and his seamen....

In those days the Stratford boy William Shakespeare was in London and had become a famous writer of plays. He must have been very fond of music, for we find he brings it into almost everything he writes. When he wants to make his audience believe in fairies (as in A Midsummer Night's Dream) he has music—pretty little fairy songs. And when he wants to make people realize how horrible witches are (as in Macbeth) he has grim witch songs. His mad people (like King Lear) sing little, disordered snatches of song in a mad sort of way. His drunken people sing bits of songs in a riotous way. His people in love sing sentimental songs.[35]

When discussing folk songs we learnt a little about Form. In Queen Elizabeth's day composers were trying to find out good 'forms' for instrumental music.

One form they found was the Variations form. They would take some jolly tune (perhaps a popular folk tune), and write it out simply; then they would write it again with elaborations, and then again with further elaborations, and so on to the end. All the great composers down to our own day have been fond of the Variations form, and it was the English Elizabethan composers who invented it.[36]

At the end of the chapter I quoted from above is a "Things to Do" section that includes the following:

1. Get two of your friends to learn this Catch with you. (It is quite easy.) Sir Toby, Sir Andrew, and the Clown sing it in Twelfth Night. [What follows is three lines of music to be sung in a round.]

Quarrelling Catch

2. Try practicing this quieter round of Shakespeare's day. Here some occasional soft singing will be in place. Try various ways of arranging soft and loud passages, with crescendos and diminuendos and settle on the way that sounds best. [37]

DRAKE AND SHAKESPEARE
CHURCH-GOING CATCH   *

It seems Miss Mason assigned books in her programmes that contained not simply stories but narration questions and activities meant to improve musical knowledge and overall music literacy. This changes everything about how we do composer study in a Charlotte Mason school or homeschool, but don't fret yet. These books are read slowly over the course of a few years. There is time to soak it in and to immerse your students in this new musical knowledge while they read the stories of great composers. I'm happy to have found these books, and I am particularly happy that many of them are available online or downloadable as PDF files. I hope this little spotlight I've given you will tide you over for now.

TELLING STORIES WITH MUSIC

When we study the works of famous composers we should take note of their use of story, too. I'm not talking about composer biographies now but about the way a composer uses music to tell a story. Just as in other subjects we use story to engage the student, here the composer has an even more intricate and difficult task—using story to engage an audience with a musical composition. This idea of stories told through music opens a whole new world to the strong listener. A student may notice (if particularly skilled in the habit of attention) that smooth motion in music can suggest calm while agitated motion suggests anger or turmoil. There are two devices at play here: legato (notes smoothly slurred together in a row) and staccato (notes played swiftly and released instantly).

A phrase in a major key sounds cheerful and lighthearted, while a phrase in a minor key sounds dramatic and dangerous. The composer can use other musical techniques, too, such as changes in tempo (fast or slow) and dynamics (loud or quiet). These are stylistic alterations that a composer can use to tell a story.

Horns playing a fanfare may evoke a hunting scene. Quiet, gentle harp music is evocative of tenderness, love, and beauty. So a composer's choice of instrument also comes into play when telling a musical story.

To recap, we have:

a) legato or staccato movement
b) major or minor key changes
c) tempo and dynamics changes
d) choice of instrument

Each of the techniques above can aid the composer in his or her quest to tell a story with musical notes on a staff. With these and other tools in the composer's arsenal, he or she can design a musical tale, complete with hero and fair lady, conflict between good and evil, rising action, climax, and resolution.

Sometimes it is easy to understand what a composer is trying to convey with a musical story. Rossini wrote his "Duetto Buffo di Due Gatti" late one night when he was constantly distracted by feuding cats screaming outside his window in the back alley. You can find this operatic duet on YouTube. It's a fantastic introduction to Rossini for children. They will not only hear wild meowing; they will also understand from the musical phrasing that these two cats are not at all happy with one another!

This is another perfect selah moment. Go find Rossini's Duetto Buffo di Due Gatti and listen to it. Can you hear the meowing? After hearing it, you may find it becomes an "ear worm" that just won't leave your brain. That's a sign of masterful composing!

At times, the composer's story is more subtle, as is the case with Schubert's *Death and the Maiden*. You may recognize this story from a twentieth century movie, *Meet Joe Black*. Death appears suddenly to a young maiden collecting firewood in the forest. He instantly falls in love with her and the subsequent battle in his heart keeps him from killing her. He eventually chooses to take an animal instead. Eternally grateful, she falls in love with Death, and they remain together for a time. He must leave, however, and in the final scene, we see that she has a photo of him on her mantle and his child in her arms.

Schubert's phrasing, choice of instruments, and use of major and minor key changes all work together to tell the story of *Death and the Maiden*, but it helps to know the story in advance as the story elements are not entirely clear to the average listener. Perhaps even more tragic than the story itself is the knowledge that Schubert wrote this quartet after learning he had contracted a terminal disease and would soon die. You can almost sense his internal anguish as you listen to this piece.

If you study *Death and the Maiden* this way, by first introducing the story and connecting your students with Schubert's own inner turmoil, you will find that your students begin to care about Schubert. They will wish they could travel back in time and save him from contracting the killer disease. A tear or two may fall as they listen to his work, knowing his life was cut short by an illness that, if contracted during our time, would have been cured by antibiotics. This caring concern is precisely what Miss Mason wanted. One of the most important aspects of a living education is that our students find something to care about. What they care about, they remember. And we want them to remember, to connect with the materials we put before them and to connect with humanity as a whole. You will find that stories like Schubert's *Death and the Maiden* will be remembered vividly.

We call this type of music that tells a story "program music" (or sometimes "programme music"). Here are a few more examples:

- Richard Strauss's *Don Quixote*
- Berlioz's *Symphonie Fantastique* (morbid nightmares)
- Tchaikovsky's *Romeo and Juliet, Swan Lake*, and *Nutcracker Suite*
- Prokofiev's *Dance of the Knights* from *Romeo and Juliet* (swords clashing, lots of drama)
- Grieg's *Peer Gynt* (pastoral scenes)
- Mussorgsky's *Pictures at an Exhibition* (music depicting a visit to an art exhibit)
- Mendelssohn's *Hebrides Overture* (you can hear the lapping of waves at the edge of Fingal's Cave)
- Debussy's *Prelude to the Afternoon of a Faun*
- Stravinsky's *Fireworks Suite*
- Vaughan Williams' *The Lark Ascending*

Beethoven said of his *Pastoral Symphony (No. 6)* "the whole work can be perceived without description—it is more an expression of feelings rather than tone-painting."[38] Despite his comments, though, you can hear bird calls, a babbling brook, a storm, etc. within the symphony. There may not have been an actual tale told, but the music is evocative of a nature scene.

When asked about the meaning of his *Sonata No. 1 in f minor*, Beethoven said, "Go read Shakespeare's *The Tempest!*" Sometimes the story is obvious, and others a bit enigmatic. If you listen to the *f minor sonata*, you may not immediately recognize the details of Shakespeare's *The Tempest*.[39] I didn't. Beethoven's comment has baffled the most distinguished reviewer throughout the ages. But we have the composer's word on the matter. This sonata, too, is story.

Another device composers often use to tell musical stories is called "leitmotif." A leitmotif is a brief, recurring musical phrase. Some composers use leitmotif to personify a character in music or to bring us back to the main theme: fleeing through a forest or picking wildflowers, for example. You can hear leitmotif in movies and television shows, too. Every time the camera swings onto Tara in *Gone With the Wind*, you hear the same characteristic musical phrase. If you are familiar with the movie, you may hear it in your mind even now. *The Lord of the Rings, Star Wars*, and other movies also have examples of leitmotif. The original example of leitmotif, however, is Wagner's famous *Ring Cycle*. In fact, Wagner is the king of program music. Listen to his "Ride of the Valkyries," "*Siegfried*'s Funeral March," "Tristan and Isolde," and "Pilgrim's Chorus." You will be immediately enveloped in story. Here is a snapshot of the primary action in "Ride of the Valkyries":

> The Valkyries are Wotan's daughters (with Erda, the earthly wisdom goddess) and chief among them is his favorite, Brünnhilde. At the beginning of Act III of *Die Walküre*, they are gathered on a mountaintop, collecting slain heroes to take to Valhalla. "The Ride of the Valkyries" on their flying horses is depicted in fiercely martial music of swirling strings and trilling woodwinds, as unison brass blaze a motif associated with Brünnhilde.[40]

This dramatic piece is a wonderful introduction to program music and leitmotif for children. They can speed across the living room on imaginary flying horses while the music blares loudly in the background. They can narrate the story of the music as they are acting it out or simply listen and enjoy the dramatic flair that is associated with Wagner's *Ring Cycle*.

This is another selah moment. Go to an online listening space and find Wagner's "Ride of the Valkyries." It is an energizing piece, filled with passion and haunting emotion. Now that you know the background—the story—I hope you will find this dramatic piece has fresh meaning.

There are many more examples of tone poems, program music, and leitmotif, primarily from the nineteenth century. As you approach each new composer, see if you can find any program music in his or her repertoire. You may be surprised at how many pieces you find. And there may be more connections than originally understood. Respighi, who orchestrated some of Rachmaninoff's piano pieces, is said to have told him that one particular Etude-Tableaux brought to mind an obscure Russian painting. Rachmaninoff looked startled and said it was the exact painting on which he had based the piece.[41]

Although there is a great deal of knowledge to be acquired when it comes to music (notation, dynamics, instrumentation, musical vocabulary, learning an instrument, sight-singing, music reading, and overall musical understanding), we will give our students a strong head start by showing them how to enjoy musical compositions as stories written in another language, understandable if not readable (yet). We have as our great example, "... Miss Mason's epoch-making discovery, the 'great avidity for knowledge in children of all ages and of every class' which is presented to them in more or less literary form."[42]

WHEN THE COMPOSER'S STORY RESIDES WITHIN THE MUSIC

We have scattered throughout history, many examples of real-life tales of woe that made it into a composer's musical story. But there is one that stands out above the rest. Our dear opera composer, Giacomo Puccini, was not exactly free of vices, one of which, unfortunately, was adultery. He had affairs with several women throughout his marriage and was once accused of yet another affair with one of his maids. This time, however, the stories were not true. The maid was horrified and eventually killed herself as a result of the scandal. Her autopsy revealed that she had died a virgin—it was only later discovered that the affair had been with her cousin.

Puccini was naturally shaken up by the innocent girl's suicide. Elvira, his wife, was found guilty of slander when it was discovered that her accusations were unfounded. Puccini paid off the girl's family to save Elvira from a jail sentence, and he was visibly changed after this chain of events. He hid away and wrote *Madama Butterfly* immediately afterward, and in sweet, innocent Butterfly's voice, you can hear the anguish of Puccini's young maid. The shame—his own shame—at this heartbreaking story shines through brilliantly. It was a crushing personal blow for Puccini, and the power of that moment on stage is palpable, perhaps partly because it bears so much truth.

We are reminded here of Miss Mason's talk of splendid failures: "It seems well to dwell at length on this subject of eccentricity, because the world loses a great deal by its splendid failures, the beautiful human beings who, through one sort of eccentricity or another, become ineffectual for the raising of the rest of us."[43] Although his story is not one to emulate, Puccini left us perhaps some of the most lyrically beautiful music of all time. I, for one, am grateful for his contribution to the wide collection of beauty and truth in the world, if not, perhaps, to its goodness.

Music is moonlight in the gloomy night of life.

—*Jean Paul Richter*

Chapter Five

Souls Rejuvenated:
Music and the Natural World

Let me lie down on the grass,
mouth open, drinking in wonder.
Let me swim in the filling pond
of notions, an ocean of delight.

Miss Mason stressed the importance of nature study, especially for young children. Making connections with the earth and everything in it, including species found in far away places and sights, sounds, and textures of the student's own place in the world, was paramount. While we may generally think of nature study as an introduction to scientific inquiry, there is more to a relationship with nature than simply understanding its function. There is great beauty in a flowing waterfall, a babbling brook, a tiny insect, even a blade of grass. A child brought up spending time outdoors, whistling tunes through a blade of grass instead of seeing grass as a utilitarian carpet on which to walk or worse, evidence of a task or chore to be done (mowing), will feel connected to the planet, even to the universe, in ways we might not ordinarily see in the average school child.

But what does this have to do with music? Nature has inspired some of the world's greatest composers to write joy-filled music, bursting with all the intensity of a planet teeming with life. And nature itself is filled with music.

Hempton (the Acoustic Ecologist) says, "Oh, grass wind. Oh, that is absolutely gorgeous, grass wind and pine wind. You know, we can go back to the writing of John Muir; he turned me on to the fact that the tone, the pitch, of the wind is a function of the length of the needle or the blade of grass. So the shorter the needle on the pine, the higher the pitch; the longer, the lower the pitch. ... There is a fundamental frequency for each habitat."[45]

Hempton analyzes acoustic energy and vibrations within nature. He is an expert noticer, a profound listener. Here he describes another of his adventures in listening:

> We're about to enter into a giant driftwood log. It's a Sitka spruce log, the same material that's used in the crafting of violins, and it has a special property where that, when the wood fibers are excited by acoustic energy — in this case, it's the sound of the ocean itself — that the fibers actually vibrate. And inside, we get to listen to nature's largest violin.[46]

May Byron tells us of the impact nature had on one of history's greatest composers, Ludwig van Beethoven. She speaks of a pianist named Charles Neate who traveled a great distance to seek the master's advice about his own compositions. Byron describes Neate's first encounter with the great composer:

> He, therefore, accepted the young man with unwonted graciousness and alacrity, looked through his compositions and gave him sound advice, and finally, thrusting away his own manuscript, proposed that they two should take a little walk, to get a breath of fresh air before further operations. They passed out into the sunlit fields. Never in all his life had Neate met a man so taken up with nature, so enrapt with the contemplation of trees, flowers, cloud, and sward. 'Nature seemed his nourishment.'[47]

In his *First Book of the Great Musicians*, Percy Scholes says, "Beethoven loved nature, and when he took a holiday he would wander about the fields and woods, thoroughly happy. ... Some people used to stare at Beethoven in the country, because he was so wild. He would rush about and wave his arms and shout his joy."[48]

Beethoven once confessed that he preferred the company of a tree to that of a man, and some of his best ideas came to him on his daily outdoor walks (the *Pastoral Symphony* among them)[49]. But Beethoven was not the only composer who was influenced by nature. Mozart said his favorite place to compose was in an open garden. In her *Story of Music and Musicians for Young Readers*, Lucy Lillie tells us:

> Old Mr. Mozart fell ill and for some time the children had to keep very quiet. The harpsichord was closed, and the brother and sister took to running about the pretty, suburban place, no doubt enjoying the respite from practicing; but even in this happy time Mozart's little brain was at work with musical compositions. The enforced idleness and freedom from care was in its way productive. He delighted to romp with Nannerl, to build up a little house of stone and moss and weeds in the garden back of their lodgings; but the undercurrent was an impulse towards musical work, mingling with his play and frolics, and finally taking definite shape, when he composed his first symphony (Opus 15). He was then in his tenth year, but in this work an amount of scientific knowledge is displayed which, taking the resources of the time into consideration, shows us what sparkling genius the boy Mozart possessed. Soon after this the father recovered, the family removed to a quaint old inn in Cornhill, London, and more concerts were advertised; but the children had their precious souvenir of that 'field-and-flower' holiday in the manuscript which was produced to the delight of the father during his convalescence...[50]

From his home in Zurich, Richard Wagner used to go on hikes into the Alps, walking among glaciers and through wooded valleys (the Sihl Valley in particular). The weather in Switzerland, with its chilly breezes and fresh, thin air, along with the vigor of life in such a climate, led Wagner to produce some of his best, most inspired works such as the "Valhalla" music in *Das Rheingold* and "Forest Murmurs" from *Siegfried*.[51]

If you close your eyes and listen to Jean Sibelius's tone poem *Tapiola*, you can almost feel the Finnish pine needles on your cheek as you struggle to walk through the intense snowstorm along with Sibelius. The score's preface reads: "Widespread they stand, the Northland's dusky forests, ancient, mysterious, brooding savage dreams; within them dwells the forest's mighty god, and wood-sprites in the gloom weave magic secrets."[52] What a remarkable tale Sibelius weaves with his orchestral music! You can feel the drudgery of each heavy footstep, as the flutes' furry snowflakes drop listlessly onto weary arms and frostbitten cheeks.

While we're on a wintry journey together, Richard Strauss's *Alpine Symphony* takes the listener through the course of one long day beginning before dawn with a blazing sunrise and onward through meadows, mountain storms, and finally, sunset.[53]

Modern English composer Frederick Delius wrote Summer Night on the River, On Hearing the First Cuckoo in Spring, A Song of Summer, The Song of the High Hills, Walk to the Paradise Garden, and Sea Drift, after a poem by Walt Whitman from his Leaves of Grass collection. Take a Selah moment and go listen to Summer Night on the River. It's haunting and beautiful, yet still retains that dissonant modern format. It's as if Delius was such a new modern composer that as he soared he still had that lush romanticism dripping from his wings.

Although Aaron Copland was born in Brooklyn, New York, he viewed the inspiration of the natural world as one of the most valuable facets of human existence. He was the great pioneer of a genre of music all his own—open prairie music, as exemplified in such pieces as *Appalachian Spring, An Outdoor Overture*, and *Billy the Kid*. If you listen to these, you may recognize them as themes from western movies or background music from commercials you have seen on television. Take a moment, a selah moment, to stop and spend some time listening to Aaron Copland themes. Some of these shows may come up in your search. (Spike Lee's He Got Game is one of them. Steinbeck's *The Red Pony* is another.)

In 1723, Vivaldi wrote twelve concertos, four of which make up his *Four Seasons*. Three of the other concertos— "Pleasure," "The Hunt," and "Storm at Sea"—also depict vibrant pastoral scenes.[54]

And how has the natural world influenced the audience's reception of the music? Beethoven's Fifth Symphony was not well received at its debut on December 22, 1808. It is thought that the harsh reviews he received had more to do with the harsh weather. German winters can reach below freezing, and both the instruments and the performers suffer when that happens. Can you imagine the world without Beethoven's Fifth? I am certainly happy that his audiences gave it another try.

Handel's *Water Music* debut was an incredible success because it was first performed outdoors on a beautiful July day by fifty of the best performers in London. The instruments remained in perfect tune, and the performers were comfortable, with a cool breeze over the water to keep them refreshed. It's a good thing this performance went well. George I commissioned it as a way to upstage his son Prince George II, who was growing weary of his father's longevity and was eager to become king. He had been throwing extravagant parties as a gesture of his grandeur, and his elderly father was displeased.

The king's lavish parade down the Thames River with his musicians aroused the curiosity of many Londoners. His subjects wanted to hear the beautiful lilting music of the great Handel, too. Picture the river loaded with barges, all filled with people dressed in their finest gowns and suits, each attempting to be more showy than the next, with the king heading the water parade. It must have been quite a spectacle. Beautiful music, birds singing, the breeze blowing gently across the water. Picture perfect.

FOR THE BIRDS

A visitor once said, "Mendelssohn and Moscheles performed actual marvels at the piano, the delicacy and lightness of both their styles reminding [me] 'of a forest full of delicious birds.'"[55] Composers have long been fascinated with birdsong and bird calls. Remember, there has not always been a way to capture them as recordings. The essence of their songs remained a thing to be experienced in the moment, something to be cherished on an early spring morning, sipping tea on the veranda or tending to flocks and fields. A sharp ear is needed for a student of nature to discern one call from another, but in those days it could be done by the average school child.

Miss Mason said, "The hearing ear comes, like good batting, with much practice; and the time will come when in a whole chorus of birds you will be able to distinguish between the different voices, and say which is the thrush, which is the blackbird, which the white-throat, which the black-cap, which the wren, which the chaffinch. Think how happy the person must be for whom every bird's note is the voice of a friend whom he knows!"[56]

Composers, in touch with their inner child listeners, began incorporating birdsong into their compositions. After all, without a way to record them, it was up to the composers of the day to reproduce them for an eager public. David Kettle of Sinfini Music says, "...composers have been fascinated by birdsong since the beginnings of classical music. Some have simply been inspired by its subtlety and beauty and have tried to emulate them in their own human creations, while others have seen birds as symbols of natural or spiritual glory."[57] Ah, symbols of spiritual glory. There is the original goal of a Charlotte Mason education revisited—our desire to step aside and allow the Holy Spirit to draw the child ever closer through the mediums of music, poetry, literature, heroic tale, scientific discovery, or artistic endeavor. Again, we see the possibilities for great joy and a touch of the divine upon a child's life.

In May 1784, Mozart taught his pet starling to sing the opening of the finale to his *Piano Concerto no. 17 in G*. Historians say he formed such a strong bond with his starling that he even held a funeral for the little thing when it died three years later.[58] Other composers were also influenced by bird calls and songs. Beethoven ended the second movement of his *Pastoral Symphony* with a short phrase for "nightingale (flute), quail (oboe) and the ubiquitous cuckoo (a pair of clarinets), for which the rest of the orchestra suddenly falls silent, as if in awe."[59]

Vivaldi's *Flute Concerto in D* (Il Gardellino) focuses on the trills and melodies of the goldfinch. Bela Bartok's *Third Piano Concerto* features the rufous-sided towhee, the Baltimore oriole, and other warblers of North Carolina. He was recuperating there after being diagnosed with a lung disorder and wrote this piece as thanks for the medical treatment he received.

As we traverse nature together, our tour would not be complete without Ralph Vaughan Williams' *The Lark Ascending*. This violin concerto depicts the English countryside as seen by a lark soaring high above the fields and woods. *The Lark Ascending* is one of the more popular classical music pieces, at least in England's national repertoire. You won't want to miss the sweet tones of the lark, especially since the skylark was the symbol Miss Mason chose for her PNEU schools, no doubt based in part on the inspired poem, "Ode to a Skylark" by Percy Shelley.[60] In fact, this would be another perfect Selah moment. If you can find Hilary Hahn's performance of *The Lark Ascending*, listen to it now, with eyes closed and heart wide open to the beauty of a soaring lark.

When we approach the vast empire of music literature available today armed with background information about each piece, we can enjoy and connect with the music in a deeper way than if we had no background knowledge whatsoever. Each motivation, every tidbit of knowledge we can grab about a composer—where he or she lived, what the weather and terrain were like there, how they affected the composer emotionally and mentally—points us to the heart of the composer. We can access the very heartbeat of the piece and, in a very real sense, walk in the composer's shoes for a while as we listen.

NARRATION AND COMPOSITION

Here's a novel idea, although it is by no means a required facet of a Charlotte Mason education. Miss Mason often had students write a narration in the style of an author like Jane Austen or as poetry in the style of Keats or Shelley. Narrating after listening to a musical composition can take the same form, at least for the older student. This can be incredibly rewarding work for a teen with musical aspirations. Once a solid understanding of notation is acquired, your student may write a short musical composition in the style of Beethoven's Für Elise, Bach's Minuet in G, etc. When it comes to writing songs about natural settings, your students may use various instruments or voices, unique melodies, rhythms, harmonies and textures. For example, summer storms bring a sense of foreboding and gloom. Tubas and cellos might convey this mood well. When the skies are clear again, joyful exuberance might be written for flutes and violins.

Before long, your students will be writing their own quartets, duets, and solo pieces with nature themes such as hurricanes, tornados, waterfalls, rainbows, spring breezes, trilling birds and trumpeting elephants. The sky is literally the limit.[61] Again, this is above and beyond the scope of Charlotte Mason composer study or music training. But it fits nicely within her larger educational tenets. And we want to provide a large room in which our students can explore and grow and learn.

Music, when soft voices die, vibrates in the memory.
            —*Percy Bysshe Shelley, "Music, when Soft Voices Die"*

Chapter Six

A Sense of Place and a Touch of Good Citizenship

If there are sounds in the music which recall the screaming of wind and cracking of
strained branches, I hope they may suggest deeper things than these at the same time.
— Arnold Bax

GEOGRAPHY IN MUSIC: A SENSE OF PLACE

Just as poets Robert Frost, William Wordsworth, Carl Sandburg, and others were all drawn to the natural world as their poetic muse, we have noticed together that certain composers were also inspired by nature. But let's take this inspiration a step further. Many artists, composers, poets, and authors are inspired by a particular place in nature rather than simply by nature as a whole. Gretchen Holbrook Gerzina, chair of the English department at Dartmouth College, says in her book about author Frances Hodgson Burnett:

> Two life-changing events contributed to the genesis of *The Secret Garden*, which was written late in her life. The first was the death of her sixteen-year-old son Lionel, who became increasingly ill in Washington while she was living away. ... The second loss was that of her beloved home Maytham Hall in Kent, in southern England, which she had leased for ten years. In 1908 the leaseholder decided to sell the grand house, and Burnett was forced to leave the home where she had spent the happiest

months of each year ... There she cultivated extensive gardens, held parties, and tamed a robin as she wrote outdoors at a table in a sheltered garden. Both the robin and the gardens made their way into *The Secret Garden*.[62]

Burnett had formed a lasting connection to Maytham Hall. It was her home. She forged fond memories there, put down roots, planted gardens, though not secret ones. Her emotional attachment to this one place was deep, and the loss of it was felt keenly. Such deep and intense relationships with the land can be seen in music, too. Edvard Grieg was so proud of his Nordic heritage that he said his music has the taste of codfish. He wrote the music for many nationalistic plays with Norwegian themes, and if ever music could depict pride and joy in a locale, it would be Grieg's *Peer Gynt*. As he said, "Norway's natural scenery has stamped itself on my creative imagination."[63]

As we learned earlier, Handel's *Water Music* was first performed in 1717 on the River Thames. A sense of place, in this case a continually moving place, created an atmosphere, a mood for the music. Location was a consideration even as he wrote these three instrumental suites. It informed his composition, and you can feel the rhythm and movement as you listen and imagine the king in his lavishly decorated barge floating and bouncing down the river to the music of the great George Frideric Handel.

Despite his adoration of his own personal Bohemian roots, Antonín Dvořák is remembered for the *New World Symphony*, which he wrote as a tribute to America. French composer Claude Debussy was inspired by Asian music, even to the point of using Eastern sounds, like pentatonic and whole tone scales, within his music. Béla Bartók spent quite a bit of time traveling throughout his native Hungary seeking out authentic folk tunes from his homeland to incorporate within his own music.

The land, its culture, and its people's way of life were incredibly influential to a number of great composers, including Aaron Copland, whose *Appalachian Spring* was mentioned in the previous chapter. We get a sense of the smell, taste, and feel of Copland's homeland from his music in ways that are hard to define precisely. Flute trills in a major key alternating with heavy brass in a minor key evoke an image of birds soaring above mountains. Light strings help us visualize prairie life, while crescendos and decrescendos remind us of the waves lapping against the sand. Unlike painting a picture on a canvas, making a film, or even painting a picture with words on a page through story, music can set you on the green earth of another place and leave you there for a short time to experience the sights, sounds, smells, and culture of a distant land. It takes extraordinary skill, talent, and ability to create art of this kind, but when you as a listener can close your eyes and soar above the Alps or wade in the shallows, you know the composer has reached his goal.

Composers often traveled to find inspiration rather than taking it from their own home or neighborhood. Felix Mendelssohn wrote his famed *Hebrides Overture* after (and during) a trip to the island of Staffa on the west coast of Scotland. Although he was incredibly seasick, the sound of the waves echoing through Fingal's Cave enchanted him. He was so moved by the scene that he scribbled a few lines of music onto a letter to his sister and mailed it immediately.

Charles Ives wrote his *Three Places in New England* as a tribute to the natural landscape of his home state of Connecticut. Benjamin Britten said that his "awareness of the struggle of men and women whose livelihood depends on the sea" informed his "Sea Interludes" from the opera *Peter Grimes*. His musical storms depict the *psycho*logical torment of *Peter Grimes*, the fisherman who was accused of killing his apprentices. In this case, one particular place near the sea—Britten's home on the sea front of Aldeburgh— lent its foreboding to the composition.[64]

Tchaikovsky was once discussing program music (remember, program music is music that tells a story) and said, "when the musician is reading a poetic work, or at the sight of a beautiful landscape, he is inflamed by enthusiasm to musically characterize the subject that fills him with ecstasy."[65] To Tchaikovsky, telling the story inspired by the landscape was one way to pour out his joyous emotions in musical form.

Many composers went on writing retreats to compose their most famous works. You can almost hear snatches of their natural surroundings within the music. Here are a few:

Jean Sibelius composed at Ainola, named after his wife Aino. His house had no indoor plumbing (he didn't want the noise to distract him while he was working) and its picturesque position on Lake Tuusula in Finland was quite inspiring.

Edvard Grieg composed at his summer villa, Troldhaugen, in Norway. He wrote in a small "composing hut" on the lake. It was painted bright Scandinavian red.

Gustav Mahler had three composing huts—one near Salzburg in Austria, another in the Dolomite mountains of Italy, and a third on the Wörthersee lake in Austria. He said, "Never did I experience more joy and peace than when I was working in my composing huts. The wonder and beauty of the natural world provided a constant source of inspiration."[66] Mahler always began composing before 6:00 a.m. and ended with a swim in the lake before lunch.

Benjamin Britten was forced to switch homes with a nearby artist after he became so famous that people refused to stop nosing around his house. The artist lived in "the Red House" which was down a lengthy driveway in Aldeburgh, Suffolk. Britten built a studio for himself there; in his words, "I've made myself a nice remote studio where I can bang away to my heart's content."[67]

In 1900, Giacomo Puccini built a villa on the lake in Torre del Lago, Italy, where he lived until 1921. He wrote his famous opera *Madama Butterfly* at this location. You can watch a short video about his retreat if you go to YouTube and search for "Puccini at Torre del Lago."[68]

Claude Debussy wrote his *La Mer* while staying at the Grand Hotel in Eastbourne, East Sussex. He was at the time having an affair with a young Jewish woman named Emma Bardac, who was also romantically connected to composers Georges Bizet and Gabriel Fauré.[69] She later married Debussy, but had daughters by both Debussy and Fauré. Check out the 1990 movie The Loves of Emma Bardac for more information on these love affairs that inspired Debussy's *La Mer*. (I have not previewed the movie, so buyer beware.)

Frederic Chopin so adored his native Poland that every polonaise and mazurka is infused with its essence. He lived half of his life in Paris and pined away for home the entire time. He was so emotionally attached to Poland that when he died, although he was buried at a cemetery in Paris, according to his final wish his heart was removed and buried at Holy Cross Church in Warsaw, Poland. Now that is a commitment to "place!"

A Touch of Good Citizenship

Charlotte Mason cared about producing good citizens, especially during the aftermath of World War I, when much of European society was in a state of turmoil and new ideals were being solidified. In England, people began to realize what was really important in life, and it was not money or success. While the topic of citizenship does not lend itself to music study per se, there are a couple of good citizens who deserve a mention here.

Leopold Stokowski

Gustav Mahler had a promising career in Vienna, conducting the Vienna Opera for a time. Even so, his compositions were all but lost to the next generation until Leopold Stokowski took the baton of the Philadelphia Orchestra in 1912. Stokowski was fearless, although some considered him impetuous and disrespectful. Perhaps this attitude gave him the courage to drag the Philadelphia Orchestra into the twentieth century by convincing the board to allow him to perform Mahler's music.

The curtain rose, and the audience was riveted. The piece was Mahler's "Symphony of a Thousand," so named because it required a thousand voices and instrumentalists to perform. No wonder the audience was so transfixed. This had never been attempted before, at least not in Philadelphia in 1916. A hearty thank-you to stubborn Leopold Stokowski, citizen of the decade, for making Mahler a household name forever. And may I suggest another selah moment? If you can find Mahler's "Symphony of a Thousand," listen to it now and try to imagine the grandeur of seeing it performed live for the very first time.

Dr. Alberto Gentili

A fragile Antonio Vivaldi struggled to return to Vienna one last time at the age of sixty-two. Destitute and in ill health, he was attempting a comeback but unfortunately died there on July 28, 1741. He received a pauper's burial on the hospital grounds, a hospital that is no longer in existence. Vivaldi's contemporaries valued him more as a violinist than as a composer, and he never would have expected to be remembered long after his death, although he chased fame as an elusive dream. But in 1926, something miraculous happened.

The staff at a boarding school in Italy discovered a large cache of old volumes in their archives. They wanted to sell them to antique dealers but needed first to have them evaluated so they would know how much to expect as payment. They called the National Library in Turin, which turned the matter over to music historian Dr. Alberto Gentili. The staff at the school sent several crates to Gentili, unsure what was in them. Imagine Gentili's surprise at finding volume upon volume of Vivaldi's works, letters, and manuscripts. He was overcome with emotion. What would he do? He had no money to purchase the volumes, but he did not want them to be divided among various antique dealers.

Gentili found a generous donor who purchased the manuscripts and donated them to the Turin Library in honor of his deceased son. By 1939, a grand celebration was held in Siena in honor of Vivaldi. His music was performed once again, and he skyrocketed to international fame. The rest, as they say, is history. Thank you, Dr. Alberto Gentili, citizen extraordinaire. We are truly grateful for your contributions to music history.

Johannes Brahms

The music of Antonín Dvořák would have been lost to us but for the generosity and friendship of another great citizen—Johannes Brahms. Many believed Brahms was a relic, a throwback to the Classical era. But he was actually quite forward-thinking. He saw in Dvořák the capacity to compose timeless works inspired by his Czech roots, much as Brahms was inspired by his Hungarian ones. Brahms even offered to leave his entire estate to Dvořák. He also served as proofreader and copy editor for Dvořák while he was in America, to expedite the publication of his work. Haydn admired Mozart, but even he did not go to the lengths Brahms did to further Dvořák floundering career. His influence helped lead the young composer to international acclaim. Without his patronage and intervention, it would never have been possible for Dvořák's work to survive. Many thanks to the irascible but generous Johannes Brahms.[70]

Richard Wagner

While we are on the subject, here's an example of poor citizenship. It has been said that Wagner, who had at one time been a friend to Felix Mendelssohn, tried to discredit him and get his music blacklisted after his death. He was jealous of Mendelssohn's musical gift, so he published secret anti-Semitic pamphlets and was successful in reducing Mendelssohn's popularity. It was not a noble moment in Wagner's life, and one hopes he came to regret his activities in due time, though there is no documented evidence to indicate that he did.

"Music is the medicine of the breaking heart.

—*Sir Aubrey Hunt*

Chapter Seven

The Storehouse of Living Ideas:
Centering Composers in Time

...The man who goes to hear a symphony not knowing what a symphony is often gets lost during the first five minutes. And the man who goes to hear Bach not knowing who he was, and what sort of music he wrote, is likely to be just as quickly bewildered and just as greatly disappointed.
                          —*Percy Scholes, The Listener's Guide to Music*

When we think of music history, I'm afraid we don't really consider the whole of history. Let me explain. From the dawn of time (no matter how long ago you think that might have been) to the music of today we have had written music for only approximately a thousand years. Think about that for a moment. A thousand years is not a very long time in the vast scope of history, is it? May Byron once said, "music is the youngest of all the arts—as compared to all others, a mere babe in arms, whose potentialities are still in the bud."[71] Hubert Parry, in his book *Studies of Great Composers*, put it this way:

> ...Music was in such a low state that as little as eight hundred years ago people had not even the means of putting down a tune in which the notes were of unequal length; and they did not dream of such things as bars till quite four hundred years nearer to our time. About

the time of our William the Conqueror they were beginning to puzzle out elementary details, and were trying to come to some sort of understanding as to how music might be put down on paper or parchment, and how sundry scales could be settled which would be fit to make music in.

That centers us a bit, doesn't it? During the time of William the Conqueror we finally had some curious fellows working out scales and notation. No one, including Parry, really knows what happened next:

> But they worked very slowly, and for a long time they did not even get so far as to find out how to make two voices go together in parts, nor even how to sing the simplest second to a tune; and some modern speculators on these subjects think that when they did discover how to do it, it was quite by accident—as if somebody was singing one tune, and somebody else for fun sang another; and as they found the effect amusing, they tried a little more of it, till by slow steps they really found out how to make a couple of voices or so sing different parts in a tolerably agreeable manner.[72]

As we consider music in its historical context, keep in mind that its history is much shorter than the whole of history. Or at least what we have to study has existed for a shorter period of time than actual music has. We have no real examples to study from the time David the shepherd boy wrote psalms with his harp by his side.

Charlotte Mason believed history should be to children a "storehouse of living ideas." And this is how she recommended a child learn about these ideas:

> Let him ... linger pleasantly over the history of a single man, a short period, until he thinks the thoughts of that man, is at home in the ways of that period. Though he is reading and thinking of the lifetime of a single man, he is really getting intimately acquainted with the history of a whole nation for a whole age.[73]

In applying this line of thinking to the study of music, we have a few options. We can learn about the time in which a composer lived, learn a bit about the geographical terrain, learn what the culture was like, who was in charge politically, whether wars were looming or battles raging. All of that background information is helpful in forming a picture of the time period and may even help us better understand the composer as a person. But there is another way to begin composer study. We can read about the composer and expand from there to his or her native surroundings and time period. I believe that is what Miss Mason intended. Her history charts for the early forms began with the child and expanded from there to the child's family, neighborhood, city, country, and eventually the world.

So we will begin with the man (or woman)—the composer, his or her life, work, and music. Then we will go from there to the historical time period and cultural surroundings—but only after we have become acquainted with the person who created the music. This enables children to develop a friendship with the person who composed the music rather than considering the music alone, devoid of the spark of the divine that came through a human mind—or worse, being given dry factual information before relationship has formed.

Let's take Jules Massenet as an example, since he is a lesser known (but magnificent) composer. Here are a few facts I found about his life's journey. Massenet was born in Montaud, France, and was best known for his operas. His music was gentle, light, and melodic—the direct opposite of Wagner's heavy, dramatic operas. He was born in 1842 and died in 1912. Those are the basic facts. Now, let's make him more personal to our students. Massenet wrote his operas with an eye toward who was going to sing them, toward his prima donnas, the stars of the time period. His wife didn't mind because, as she said, it was better that he was giving them operas than fine jewels.

Was he a philanderer? We don't yet know, but now we are curious about his character after reading what his wife said about him. We are also getting to know Massenet the man a bit better, right? Massenet won the Prix de Rome three years in a row and traveled extensively. He met and became friends with Franz Liszt during this time. He returned to Paris to fight in the siege of 1870 during the Franco-Prussian war. Aha! Now we have some history to look up and a friendship with a fellow composer to learn about. We were simply getting acquainted with the man, Massenet. And now we can look into the history of the Franco-Prussian war, learn about France during Massenet's time, and look up what the Prix de Rome was. (It was a group of scholarships granted by the French government to young French artists so they could study at the French Academy in Rome. Prix de Rome scholarships were awarded between 1663 and 1968.)

Most music appreciation courses take students on a journey through time, taking note of each composer's place in history. We may eventually learn who was leading the composer's country, what wars were taking place, and in some cases what political affiliations the composer had. This background information not only allows our students to better connect with the composer, but also offers us a treasured glimpse into the society of the time period, its flaws, beliefs, how its citizens spent their time, what occupations were respected most, and how musicians were treated.

Some composers left more information about themselves and their personal beliefs than others did. I'm thinking here of Beethoven and his *Eroica Symphony*, which Beethoven originally dedicated to Napoleon, only to scratch through the dedication in disgust after Napoleon made himself emperor. Ferdinand Ries recorded Beethoven as saying the following about Napoleon in 1804:

> So he is no more than a common mortal! Now, too, he will tread under foot all the rights of man, indulge only his ambition; now he will think himself superior to all men, become a tyrant![74]

Ries tells us that Beethoven then ripped out the first page of his symphony, the page that had the written dedication on it. He later rewrote the page, dedicating his symphony to all heroes (eroica means "heroic") instead of to Napoleon.

Richard Wagner's music is heavy, full, and powerful. Although many would like to forget the impact Hitler had on German history, Wagner was Hitler's favorite composer and to many, there is a stigma attached to Wagner's music. Wagner's own anti-Semitic beliefs have only added to the problem. Still, his music is aurally stunning. You can feel the intensity and power of his "Ride of the Valkyries." He created an entirely new genre of opera, refusing to write in the Italian style when it was possible to create something purely German. He was tied to the land of Germany, and to be fair, since he died in 1883, he could not have known how far Hitler's hatred of the Jewish people would take him. Wagner's heart swelled with German pride, and it showed.

Most music historians house composers within the framework of designated time periods: Medieval/Renaissance, Baroque, Classical, Romantic, and Modern. There are subcategories within each broader one, but most of the people we think of as great composers were Baroque, Classical, or Romantic. Which time period do you think gave us the most popular composers? You may be surprised to find that the Romantic period brought us much of the music we recognize today—and yet, we generally stereotype all symphonic music as "classical."

Once you begin your journey of careful listening, you will soon find yourself able to distinguish between time periods. German Baroque music is often heavier, with more brass and fanfare, while Italian Baroque music is less dramatic and more melodic. Classical music, overall, is less dense and more elegant, although it is by no means light on dramatic flair. There is more rhythmic variation in Classical music than in Baroque, too. Germans once again top the list of Classical composers. These nuances in style are a reflection of the culture of the time period.

Romantic music is emotional and almost always carries a message, even if it is a lighthearted message (think Rossini's Duet for Two Cats). Someone recently commented after posting a Schubert video on YouTube, "I hope you like the lightness and giggling motives of Schubert's #5 Symphony." It's true—the emotional silliness of Romantic music is one reason it is so frequently used as background for animated cartoons and Hollywood movies. Romantic music is also more culturally and geographically diverse than its predecessors. Polish, French, and Russian composers became popular during this time period, and rightly so. Where would be we without Chopin, Bizet, and Tchaikovsky?

And what about Modern music? It is generally thought of as a mixture of atonal dissonance, experimentation, and even silence. If you try not to take it too seriously, you will enjoy learning about this time period, but keep in mind that there have been composers whose work hearkens back to previous historical eras during every time period. So there are modern composers whose work sounds more baroque than modern. And some of the romantics added in modern elements to their works as a way to sort of test the waters of this new dissonant sound.

We believe children are born persons, so we should also remember that every individual composer is uniquely gifted by God to create what He wanted created. They should never be pigeonholed or judged within certain specific parameters based on when they lived, although when you listen to John Cage you might wonder just what God had in mind.

Here is the short list of famous composers, by time period. There is some overlap, especially in reference to Paganini and Schubert. Paganini is more a Romantic composer than a Classical one, and Schubert seems just the opposite!

BAROQUE

Claudio Monteverdi

Johann Pachelbel

Arcangelo Corelli

Antonio Vivaldi

Domenico Scarlatti

Johann Sebastian Bach

George Frideric Handel

CLASSICAL

Joseph Haydn

Wolfgang Amadeus Mozart

Ludwig van Beethoven

NiccolòLuigi Cherubini

Luigi Boccherini

Karl Ditters von Dittersdorf

Christoph Gluck

William Sterndale Bennett

Nicolo Paganini

ROMANTIC

Franz Schubert

Gioachino Rossini

Hector Berlioz

Felix Mendelssohn

Frédéric Chopin

Robert Schumann

Franz Liszt

Richard Wagner

Giuseppe Verdi

Johannes Brahms

Modest Mussorgsky

Camille Saint-Saëns

Georges Bizet

Pyotr Ilyich Tchaikovsky

Antonín Dvořák

Edvard Grieg

Giacomo Puccini

Nikolai Rimsky-Korsakov

Sergei Rachmaninoff

MODERN

Erik Satie

Gabriel Fauré

Frederick Delius

Dmitri Shostakovich

Gustav Mahler

Igor Stravinsky

Claude Debussy

Béla Bartók

Arnold Schoenberg

Philip Glass

Music can noble hints impart,
Engender fury, kindle love;
With unsuspected eloquence can move
And manage all the man with secret art.
            —*Joseph Addison, "A Song for St. Cecilia's Day at Oxford"*

Chapter Eight

A Broad Feast in a Large Room:
Intimate Glimpses of the World's Greatest Composers

The discovery of song and the creation of musical instruments both owe their origin to a human impulse which lies much deeper than conscious intention.
—Richard Baker

I'd like to present you with a brief glimpse of a few of the historical time periods we generally use to organize important composers, artists, sculptors, inventors, and architects. In other words, let me furnish your House of Mind so that when you listen to the music of the past you will have a ready space for it to land. We will discuss the Medieval and Renaissance time periods in a later chapter, so I will leave you to look up Hildegard of Bingen, Guillaume Dufay, Thomas Tallis, William Byrd, and Giovanni Pierluigi da Palestrina.

BAROQUE MUSIC (1600–1750)

During the Baroque period, European monarchies were at their height. All the pomp and pageantry we've seen in movies or read about in books appeared in Baroque music, possibly because many composers were court composers who did the bidding of their king, prince, or other noble patron.

Composers wrote pieces for national holidays, for celebrations, or merely to make the king look particularly great and powerful to his enemies.

When we consider Claudio Monteverdi, Johann Pachelbel, Arcangelo Corelli, Henry Purcell, and Domenico Scarlatti—all Baroque composers—we do not tend to place them in the same quality category as Vivaldi, Bach, and Handel (also considered Baroque). But they all played a part in the sweeping changes that took place during the time period.

The 1600s began with the death of Queen Elizabeth I. It was the era of Galileo and the King James Bible, lavish architecture and art, beginning with intricacy and grandeur and ending with the more flowery, graceful, and decorative art of the Rococo Period—Watteau, Boucher, Fragonard, Gainsborough. In Britain, we saw the first Chippendale furniture. In the New World, Jamestown was settled in Virginia, and the Pilgrims arrived in Massachusetts. Trade across the Atlantic began, and if you could bear the journey, great opportunities awaited settlers in the Americas. The pace quickened. Expectations rose. Western Europe was ablaze with news of a new land and the riches, spices, and cultures yet to be discovered.

Louis XIV, the Sun King, reigned in France, and the Salem Witch Trials marked the end of the seventeenth century in the New World. Drama and excitement were in the air, almost tangible. Naturally the music of the time reflected all these historical events. Catholics and Protestants were locked in doctrinal battle, and music was but one of their many battlefields. Handel wrote his Messiah, and Vivaldi wrote Catholic choral music for angelic young nuns. This artistic innovation and growth begun during the Renaissance, continued until the Age of Revolution when war dialed down the burgeoning artistic prowess once again.

CLAUDIO MONTEVERDI

Monteverdi played the viola da gamba (an early form of violin). He was an inventive composer and wrote one of the very first operas. He was also a Catholic priest.

JOHANN PACHELBEL

Pachelbel was a German organist, teacher, and composer of both sacred and secular music. He is best known for his *Canon in D*. I'm sure you've heard it, but if not, take a selah moment to find it and listen to it right away. Pachelbel's choral music had rich instrumentation compared to previous time periods. He also wrote harpsichord music.

ARCANGELO CORELLI

Arcangelo Corelli was an Italian composer best remembered for his *Christmas Concerto*. His music is elegant and refined compared to that of most Baroque composers.

HENRY PURCELL

English composer Henry Purcell wrote secular music set to mythic themes, anthems, hymns, and more. Benjamin Britten borrowed generously from Purcell's work for his *Young Person's Guide to the Orchestra* and *A Midsummer Night's Dream*.

DOMENICO SCARLATTI

Scarlatti was born in Naples, Italy, but he spent the last twenty-five years of his life in Portugal where he taught harpsichord to the princess (later queen) of Spain. It has been recorded that Cardinal Ottoboni in Rome set up a contest of skill between Scarlatti and Handel on the harpsichord. Scarlatti won the challenge, although it was understood that Handel reigned supreme on the organ. When asked about Handel's skill, Scarlatti crossed himself in reverence to the great master.

GEORGE FRIDERIC HANDEL

Handel had to practice in secret as a child because his father was determined that he should find an occupation that would provide a decent living—and music was not that occupation. I heard something similar from my own father when I was young, although I was still given piano lessons after I begged for them. Handel was a law student for a while. He wanted to please his father, but his adoration of music would not lie dormant for long.

Little-known fact about Handel: in 1726, he became a British citizen. He loved living in London and wanted to make it his permanent home. Handel stopped writing operas because they were not in style in England at the time. I still wonder what glorious operas he might have composed had he chosen to live in Italy instead of England. The world will never know because Handel turned his attention to oratorios instead. And would we have his great Messiah if he had not left opera composing? This is the influence a culture can have on a composer.

ANTONIO VIVALDI

Vivaldi began his career writing music for orphan girls at a home for abandoned children. His *Four Seasons* are a staple for listeners today, but during his own time he was not popular as a composer (as we learned in the section on citizenship). He was a talented violinist and also a Catholic priest.

JOHANN SEBASTIAN BACH

Bach died in 1750, having achieved some limited notoriety as an organist. It was not until his music was revived in the early part of the nineteenth century that he achieved fame. We owe a great debt to Mozart, Beethoven, Chopin, Schumann, and Mendelssohn for rediscovering Bach's counterpoint and style and insisting on performing it. They admired his keyboard work, and Beethoven described him as the "original father of harmony."[75]

CLASSICAL MUSIC (1750–1820)

During the Classical period, composers withdrew from the ornamental, overly dramatic style of the Baroque period and headed toward (and back to) what they perceived as the cleaner, clearer classical style of ancient Greece. Clarity and form replaced heaviness and complexity. There was more variance in tempo, and the music contained more staccato (quick, brief) notes than previous music did. If you compared the music of these two time periods to dancing, perhaps Baroque music would be a dramatic tango and Classical music would be a fox trot—lighter and more cheerful.

The roots of the Classical period coincided with the unearthing of Pompeii and Herculaneum in Greece. These discoveries brought about a revival of ancient architecture and a return to simplicity within the arts in general. Simplicity and symmetry replaced ornamentation, much as simple columns replaced the ornate spires of gothic cathedrals.

Newton's physics, the intellectual and philosophical pursuits of Bacon, Descartes, Locke, Kant, Montesquieu, and Rousseau—all of these "enlightened" men drove the culture toward valuing intellect above spirituality. In their intense effort to explain the meaning of life and extricate a captive society from the monarchies that enslaved them, they left much of society devoid of meaning because without the life of the spirit, all is madness and chaos.

Despite the massive (and often bloody) revolutions, the Classical period gave us such great composers as Haydn, Mozart, Paganini, and Beethoven and such magnificent artists as Jacques Louis David, William Hogarth, and Francisco Goya. The Brandenburg Gate in Berlin was modeled after classical Athens, and George Washington's Mount Vernon had a similar classical design.

In literature, authors from the Classical era include Voltaire (Candide), Jonathan Swift (Gulliver's Travels), Daniel Defoe (Robinson Crusoe), and Henry Fielding (Tom Jones). Poet Alexander Pope inspired a young slave girl named Phyllis Wheatley to write couplets about the cause of freedom both for the new world and for her own race.

By the late eighteenth century, the Great Awakening shook the new world and drove its people to their knees in repentance. Faith was again, if not supreme, at least the equal of reason. A rare season of hymn writing arose during this time, which we will explore in more detail in a later chapter. For now, here are a few significant facts about our dearest composers of the Classical age.

Franz Joseph Haydn

Austrian-born Franz Joseph Haydn was a contemporary of Mozart's. Beethoven was a bit younger—he was Haydn's student. Haydn's father was a wheelwright, his mother a cook. When he showed musical promise, they sent him to live with a cousin who was a choirmaster. Haydn left his childhood home when he was only six years old. After leaving, he returned only for occasional short visits. Although Haydn married, his wife wasn't interested in his music at all. In fact, she often used his compositions to line her pastry pans.

Haydn was considered the father of Classical music. He was even called "Papa Haydn" by those who revered him (obviously, his wife was not one of them).

Wolfgang Amadeus Mozart

Mozart deserves his own book, or at least his own chapter in this book. Haydn wrote of him, "posterity will not see such a talent again in a hundred years." He was right. But talent aside, and as we are interested in making connections between the culture and the people of a certain time period, Mozart is a conundrum. He wrote elegant, refined music—perfectly exemplifying the Classical time period—but as a German/Austrian who despised the aristocracy, he used scatological humor in his conversations and letters to family and friends. Now, to fully understand this side of dear Mozart, we must take a peek at the ugly underbelly of German folklore, which had a rather large fascination with the act of defecation. Yes, that's right. Poop.

Thin, pale, with wispy blonde hair and a soft tenor voice, Mozart might have appeared genteel. He dressed in high fashion for his time. He had good manners. But when he pointed out the aristocrats at one of his concerts in 1777, he called them "the Princess Stinkmess, and the two Princes Potbelly von Pigtail."[76] And that was mild. Mozart often used wordplays in German to create crude jokes for his family and closest friends.

Before we despise Mozart too much for being low-minded, there is evidence that Martin Luther also employed scatological humor, as did Goethe and other Germans of the time period.[77] I think this is one area we're just going to have to forget we ever learned about as we close our eyes and enjoy Mozart's lovely music.

Ludwig van Beethoven

Ludwig van Beethoven was fifteen years younger than Mozart. He was the second of seven children, but only Ludwig and two younger brothers survived to adulthood. Beethoven was a commoner. Early in life, his appearance was tidy, as were his manners. But soon his alcoholic father was so far gone that Ludwig had to raise his two younger brothers himself, playing viola for cash and seeking injunctions against his father to garnish his wages and have them sent straight to Ludwig for the boys' care. If he lost interest in proper manners and hygiene, can we not forgive him for these faults when he was such a responsible elder brother?

Ludwig fell in love with three different women over the course of his lifetime, all aristocrats who were not permitted to marry such a lowly commoner (I'm thinking he got the last laugh there). He dedicated his Moonlight Sonata to one of them, Josephine Brunsvik, and he dedicated his "Für Elise" to another, Therese Malfatti. Unfortunate in love, and penniless after caring for his younger brothers, he began composing in earnest. Some have said his greatest symphonies were composed during these seasons of intense adversity.

Although Beethoven may have suffered from bipolar depression, his pronounced irritability later in life may also have been the result of a chronic abdominal issue and his impending deafness. He could be moody, storming out of a performance if he heard chatting in the audience. But such joy came out of the inspired mind of this great composer, and he was faced with such crippling obstacles, that he stands with only a few others as one of the greatest composers of all time.

NICOLO PAGANINI

Nicolò Paganini, whose music seemed more Romantic than Classical, was not only a wonderful composer but also a brilliant violinist. He played with such force and skill that one concert-goer was convinced he got his power by selling his soul to the devil. You may have heard of Paganini's amazing violin technique, but did you know it was probably caused by Ehlers-Danlos syndrome?[78] This disorder's main characteristic involves the loosening of the connective tissue between small joints in the body. Paganini could stretch and reach for notes no other violinist could possibly play. Some of his compositions require greater skill than most people could ever possess, even by today's standards. His music is passionate and beautiful. If you have never heard Paganini's violin music, you are in for a real treat. It is extraordinary. It is also more Romantic than Classical in nature, but if we are to go by date only, he would be considered a Classical composer.

A handful of lesser known Classical composers rounds out our list. They are Luigi Cherubini, Luigi Boccherini, Karl Ditters von Dittersdorf, Christoph Gluck, and William Sterndale Bennett.

Bennett was renowned not only as a composer and performer (a pianist) but also as a teacher at the Royal Academy of Music. He impressed Mendelssohn, was a friend to Schumann, trained Hubert Parry, whose books Miss Mason used in her curricula, and was even knighted and buried at Westminster Abbey. Why have most of us never heard of William Sterndale Bennett? I have no idea. Take a moment to pause (Selah), find, and listen to his Piano Concerto No. 1 in d Minor.

ROMANTIC MUSIC (1820–1900)

The Romantic era was a reaction to the Classical period's season of intellectual effort, and I believe a welcome one. Beauty and relationship cannot be held down for long without a strong backlash. People long for love, meaning, and beauty. We need art and music in order to be fully alive and happy. The Romantic composers again turned to the past for inspiration, this time to the

Medieval period and its heroes of chivalry, its long poems and tales of love and woe. Who says chivalry is dead? The Romantics revived it with all the tenderness and gentleness of a damsel in distress waving toward her knight in shining armor. But what does this look like in a musical format?

Layers of texture and melody in major keys evoke an emotional response and connection that is missing or less clear in the Classical music of the previous era. The Romantic era also saw greater dynamic contrast, freer tempos, more complex harmonies, and more adventurous orchestration. Listen to Tchaikovsky's *Romeo and Juliet* for its sweeping romance. You can hear it in the crescendo of the main theme. Or listen to the third movement of Brahms' third symphony. Again, you will hear crescendos and decrescendos and increasing tension and release from minor keys to major ones. In fact, take a selah moment to do that right now. Tchaikovsky's main *Romeo and Juliet* theme will stay with you long after you hear it. And unlike other "ear worms" that annoy us, this one will be a welcome change!

There are so many romantic composers that deserve mention, but for the sake of space, here are a few chart-topping favorites: Franz Schubert, Gioachino Rossini, Felix Mendelssohn, Frédéric Chopin, Johannes Brahms, Georges Bizet, Pyotr Ilyich Tchaikovsky, Antonín Dvořák, Edvard Grieg, Giacomo Puccini, Nikolai Rimsky-Korsakov, Sergei Rachmaninoff. I wish we could sit down together with a cup of tea and listen to the music of every one of these brilliant, gifted composers. Since we cannot, I hope you will look them up and dig for *yourselves* to find the rich cultural treasure that allowed these composers to produce the inspiring works they left us. Here are a few:

Gioachino Rossini

Gioachino Rossini's father was a horn player and a slaughterhouse inspector. His mother was an opera singer and the daughter of a baker. So you can understand why Rossini's childhood was somewhat disjointed. His father was jailed by Napoleon's troops, leaving Rossini in the care of his mother, who moved them to Bologna where she became a singer in the theater. When his father returned, he was frequently playing with orchestras, leaving young Gioachino with a pork butcher who was a friend of the family. At one point, he was able to take harpsichord lessons—from a narcoleptic beer peddler. Gioachino was later apprenticed to a blacksmith, and yet he somehow managed to learn to play the cello. Welcome to nineteenth-century Italian culture! Rossini is best remembered for his *William Tell* overture and his opera *The Barber of Seville.*

FREDERIC CHOPIN

Frédéric Chopin was from Poland, but he composed and performed in Paris as well, bringing his nationalistic Polish music to the masses. Unlike Mozart and Beethoven, Chopin was reserved, fragile, tender, and reclusive. He preferred performing at small parties to large recitals or concerts. He wrote primarily for the piano, and among his most memorable pieces are the Minute Waltz and his Nocturne in E flat major, op. 9, no. 2.. Don't miss his *funeral march* from the *Piano Sonata in B*, his *Heroic Polonaise*, and his *Revolutionary Etude*. If you can, take a selah moment and go listen to a few of these pieces. They are remarkable and completely different from one another.

JOHANNES BRAHMS

Until his voice finally changed at age twenty-four (yes, that late!) Johannes Brahms was a short, blonde-haired soprano. He grew a beard once he was able and kept it for the rest of his life. (Wouldn't you?) Here are a few more quirky insights into Brahms' personality. He had no children of his own and never married. He loved playing with toy soldiers, had frogs for pets, once conducted an outdoor concert while standing in a tree, adored coffee (Viennese roast), suffered from migraines, and was nearsighted. He hated dentists. He lost all his teeth and had to wear dentures, so that may have had a little something to do with it. His one great romantic love was for Clara Schumann, who was a brilliant composer and performer herself. Brahms was more than a decade younger than Clara, and although they were deeply in love, they never married.

Brahms is best known for his famous lullaby, but you may also have heard his Hungarian Dance no. 5 and the third movement from his Symphony no.

3. His music is lilting and sweet. Brahms was wealthy and famous during his lifetime and very generous. (Remember what he did for Dvořák?)

Pyotr Ilyich Tchaikovsky

Tchaikovsky began improvising on the piano when he was only four years old, but he grew up to become a lawyer by trade. That didn't last long. Once he began composing, there was no end to the delight he brought first to his native Russia and later, the world.

Most people can name at least one of Tchaikovsky's famous compositions. Can you? It was *Swan Lake* that propelled him to fame originally, followed by the 1812 Overture, *Sleeping Beauty*, *The Nutcracker*, and *Romeo and Juliet*. An 1891 Carnegie Hall program noted that he, Brahms, and Saint-Saëns were the three greatest living musicians, and one critic went so far as to call him a music "lord."[79]

He lived for only fifty-three years, living sixteen years beyond his suicide attempt in 1877. He died of cholera, leaving behind a legacy of beauty and joy for all humanity. From the depths of his emotional despair, Tchaikovsky brought us beauty for ashes. And he may never have understood that the Holy Spirit Who hovered over the waters at creation was at work in his life, shining from within him, bringing joy to endless generations to come.

Modern Music and Beyond (1901–Present)

The music we consider Modern today was primarily a reaction to the lush delicacy attributed to the Romantic period. You could say the composers of the time—the early twentieth-century—were weary of lilting melodies and yearning for freedom from form and for more experimentation. There were a few composers who bridged the gap between the Romantic and Modern time periods. Gabriel Fauré, Claude Debussy, Erik Satie, and Maurice Ravel were considered Late Romantic or Impressionist composers. (Debussy, however, disliked the term Impressionism. He said, "what the imbeciles call 'impressionism' is a term which is as poorly used as possible, particularly by art critics.")[80]

Modern music covers a vast array of styles, from electronic, synthesized music to atonal music that does not follow a particular scale. What is typically considered Modern music is sometimes called "experimental music" to differentiate it from Late Romantic or Impressionistic compositions. The use of dissonance and widely varying rhythms and form characterize Modern music. It is often highly expressive and is sometimes also known as Expressionist music rather than experimental music. Mahler, Stravinsky, Bartok, and Ives are Expressionist composers. Their music is less experimental than some composers of the time period.

By 1930, optimism gave way to pessimism and Postmodern music was born. Its hero, John Cage, wrote the famous 4'33" which consists of total silence for four minutes and thirty-three seconds. The orchestra sits silently. The conductor stands at the podium without moving. "But anyone could have written that piece!" you say. And that would be the truth!

Some Modern composers looked to the past, and others were somewhat futuristic, always pressing forward and experimenting, applying new technologies and methods to their work. Later Modern composers include Phillip Glass, Elliott Carter, and Dmitri Shostakovich.

GUSTAV MAHLER

Gustav Mahler was my father's favorite composer, but I have to admit I have not warmed up to him so readily. He ushered in the Modern period in music, though, so any study of the time period would have to include his contribution.

IGOR STRAVINSKY

Russian composer Igor Stravinsky, later a naturalized French and American citizen, was a composer, pianist, and conductor. He is most remembered for his *Firebird Suite* and *The Rite of Spring*. His music is diverse and expressionistic. He was considered revolutionary in his time and was continually pushing at the boundaries, creating works filled with rhythmic energy that tiptoed around the edges of dissonance. He was taught by Nikolai Rimsky-Korsakov. He met Pablo Picasso in 1917; in his words, "in a whirlpool of artistic enthusiasm and excitement I at last met Picasso."[81] They became immediate friends.

Claude Debussy

Claude Debussy grew up in poverty in a suburb of Paris and was suddenly and surprisingly plucked from his family to travel and perform duets with a Russian millionairess and her children. She had been impressed by his musical prowess. He moved into her mansion where he studied until winning the Grand Prix de Rome. He must have felt just like Cinderella! Debussy was influenced by the high drama of Wagner's operas, but his music is haunting, poetic, and mildly dissonant.

Experiencing the music of the past while considering where it is placed in history can enrich your music study in immeasurable ways. Suddenly, the drama of a Beethoven symphony smells like war and revolution. Puccini becomes an Italian feast with wine and song. Prokofiev entertains our children with tales about wolves, while elegant minuets and waltzes remind us that Classical aristocracy has replaced monarchy and the era of revolution has ended. Our eyes close and we are taken away to romantic realms, to halls of mountain kings and Fingal's Cave, to days of courage and nobility. This is what music can do to a soul.

"Music is love in search of a word."

—*Sidney Lanier*

Chapter Nine

The Science of Relations:
Apperception, Foundational Knowledge,
and Other Pivotal Concepts

Most people use music as a couch; they want to be pillowed on it, relaxed and
consoled for the stress of daily living. But serious music was never meant to
be soporific.

—Aaron Copland, "A Modernist Defends Modern Music"

Renaissance. The word itself means "rebirth," and the time period
associated with it brought a rebirth of classical learning in science,
art, sculpture, architecture, and more. Music was still somewhat
relegated to the church aside from the madrigals sung at court and with gusto
down at the local pub. Still, the glorious awakening to the arts that we know
of as the Renaissance brought such enthusiasm and excitement that in any
discussion of the composers of the age—Guillaume Dufay, Thomas Tallis,
William Byrd, and Giovanni Pierluigi da Palestrina—we should secure them
nicely into the flush of newness that was their time period. What exactly was
the artistic and creative backdrop for these Renaissance composers?

Lorenzo Ghiberti's baptistery doors, Filippo Brunelleschi's dome, and
Donatello's sculpture ushered in the early Renaissance in Florence, followed
by the magnificent three: Da Vinci, Michelangelo, and Raphael. Giorgione
and Titian, Van Eyk and Dürer produced glorious paintings and etchings

during this time period. The air was electric with new inventions and new ideas: eyeglasses, the printing press, the flushing toilet, microscopes, telescopes, submarines, rifles, bottled beer, the spinet piano, the cuckoo clock, champagne, and wallpaper. Petrarch, Shakespeare, and Spenser dominated literature during the Renaissance, but there were many more poets and composers writing love sonnets and wooing young ladies with them. This is the rich environment in which Renaissance composers created their masterpieces. And this is only the European landscape. Delving deeper, you will also find a rich Muslim heritage in Spain and the Arab world. In fact, modern flamenco music may have begun in part as post-medieval Muslim music in Spain.

Before we tie all this information up neatly and package it as a unit study curriculum, which Miss Mason would never have wanted us to do, it's important that we remember we are only providing it for the sake of cultural literacy for our students, and so that they will have some knowledge about the art, architecture, and ideas of the past to help them understand what each composer's life and work was like and what impacted it. We talked about this earlier. We even discussed whether to include this knowledge after getting to know the composer as a person, spreading outward to his or her city, country, and culture, or whether we should instead begin with the outlying culture of the time and journey in toward the composer afterward. But that was a discussion about what to include and where to include it. Now I want to talk about why it's so crucial that we provide it.

Background information is important for several reasons, but the primary one relies on the research of Miss Mason's friend and associate in education, Thomas Rooper. He wrote a book called *A Pot of Green Feathers*, which details the value of laying out foundational information for children. If you show students who have never seen a garden a vase filled with vibrant green ferns and ask them what they see, they may say "a vase full of ferns" or they may say "a pot of green feathers." Without the vocabulary and background knowledge necessary to interpret what they see, students will be perpetually at a loss when it comes to learning in any new field of endeavor. This is true of all subjects, but it is of primary importance when it comes to music, which is both subjective (because appreciation is relative, and the feelings it evokes vary) and objective (because music follows a template and rules).

Children cannot know what they do not know. Knowledge builds upon itself. This is why children who have not been read to early in life and who have been less privileged in general than the average middle-class child will need more time and experience before they can cognitively understand the beauty, truth, and in fact, all of the educational subjects around them. They are perfectly capable, as Miss Mason discovered for herself when she educated children from impoverished coal mining families. They simply have no furnishings within their house of mind on which to lay these new thoughts down.

In *A Pot of Green Feathers*, Rooper calls the proper taking in of new information apperception, though he was not the first to use the term. We perceive what certain things are because we have a basic understanding about them already or at least something on which to hang new knowledge and information. The importance of apperception cannot be underestimated. It is the difference between the ability to see a vase of ferns and the lack that only allows a student to see a pot of green feathers. We want to set the table for a rich and varied feast, but maybe we need to work up to that by serving a couple of new dishes at dinner now and again until we find the student is ready to digest something richer on a regular basis.

We see apperception deficits in our schools, where they hinder students from grasping the concepts and ideas they are presented with. How do you teach a native Spanish speaker to read when they don't know how to sound out the letters *h* and *j*? How do you explain to a sixth grader who has just arrived traumatized from Sudan the nuanced differences between the words *horrible, horrific, horrendous, and atrocious? Doubtful* and *dubious? Enlightenment* and *illumination?* How can we expect our urban students from low-income areas to understand the importance of these nuances between words when they have not been read to regularly because their parents both work long hours to support the family?

Students need to know why it is important that they learn about music— what purpose it will serve for their lives. What do we expect to accomplish in providing them with a cultured existence full of art, music, architecture, and sculpture? Do they need this exposure to fully live? Is it really all that important?

I think Miss Mason would offer an emphatic yes. The benefit of learning about all aspects of the arts and sciences, mathematics and history, is that it encourages us to form relationships with people, things, and events of the past, present, and future—to understand our universe and to fully grasp our place within the broader scheme. That is what Miss Mason meant by "the Science of Relations."

Now, here things get a little fuzzy. Miss Mason seems to disagree with Rooper about the importance of apperception, yet he was one of her frequent writers for *The Parents' Review* and a close, trusted friend. But maybe she's merely making the distinction between what relationship is and is not. She says:

> On what does Fulness of Living depend?—What is education after all? An answer lies in the phrase—Education is the Science of Relations. I do not use this phrase, let me say once more, in the Herbartian sense— that things are related to each other, and we must be careful to pack the right things in together, so that, having got into the brain of a boy, each thing may fasten on its cousins, and together they may make a strong clique or 'apperception mass.' What we are concerned with is the fact that we personally have relations with all that there is in the present, all that there has been in the past, and all that there will be in the future—with all above us and all about us—and that fulness of living, expansion, expression, and serviceableness, for each of us, depend upon how far we apprehend these relationships and how many of them we lay hold of.[82]

Miss Mason was not against apperception itself, as an aid to apprehending all that the world has to offer a child. I believe she was trying to tell us just how important it is to open a wide feast of living ideas to our students, to expand their world and reveal through books and objects (and music and art) the greatness that is our entire world, from beginning to end, across the globe, and even above and below it (and all the things that are spiritually discerned within it). But that can only be done when the "apperception mass" is in place.

I admit I originally believed the Science of Relations could be defined as providing children with books that will segue nicely and tie in certain concepts with other concepts so that they will gain a stronger understanding of the subject at hand. It does begin to resemble a unit study when you look at it that way, doesn't it? But Miss Mason wanted every child to partake of the "fullness of living" that was the right of every human being. These were the relations she wanted them to have. And that includes children of every socioeconomic level, every culture—every single child. A rich heritage of learning was to be opened up to everyone.

What a novel concept at a time when children were only recently sprung from their sweat shop duties or industrial work in factories. But children need some background knowledge in order to fully appreciate the new ideas that we present to them—knowledge that includes not only the cultural backdrop of a composer's life and place and influences but also how music actually works, how it functions, and how we listen to it—how the brain takes in music and ingests it with sensitivity.

UNDERSTANDING SOUND

There is so much we take for granted when we listen to and study great music. The science involved is intricate and extraordinary. Here is another aspect of the student–music relationship that we have yet to unpack fully. For example, what is sound? We know that sound comes to the ear in waves caused by an external force emitting energy in the form of a vibration. It sounds so clinical, but that is the essence of what we experience, from a scientific standpoint, when we listen to music.

Add to that the acoustics of a particular space. If you scream at the top of your voice in a large empty room with a high ceiling, the sound of your voice would be very different than if you screamed in a smaller, furnished room filled with people. Sound waves move through the air in a way that's similar to how a thrust of energy moves through a child's slinky toy. Imagine dozens of slinkies toppling over desks, people, and against walls. This is essentially what happens when sound waves move through different performance spaces.

There are subtle differences between instruments that alter the type of sound they make by altering the types of vibrations they create. A violin is smaller and its tone higher than a viola or cello, for example. A flute has an open hole that you blow across, while a clarinet has a thin, flat mouthpiece with a reed that you blow past. Some wind instruments have curved ends and some have straight ends. Some are larger than others. The timbre (the "color" or unique quality of the sound) is different on different instruments. The texture varies. The tone can be harsh or gentle. Contrast a cymbal with a harp. These differences create diversity within the musical experience. They are important tools for a composer, and they must be mastered or at least understood if the composer wants to use them well. They are also important for the listener, because these differences in sound are one of the ways that composers tell stories or communicate emotion through their music. It's fascinating to look at how each instrument makes music, the history behind its development, the science of how it works. This, too, is music study.

Miss Mason turned over a substantial amount of trust to others when it came to music education. Upon her recommendation, her students read *The Listener's Guide to Music* by Alfred P. Scholes. This book contains a detailed look at instrumentation and composition. It's available online as a digital download and I would definitely put it on a must-buy composer study list.[83] In the original PNEU programmes, Scholes' book is used over the course of a few years as a supplement to the composers studied each term. I have reprinted the PNEU programmes in appendix A. You can see from them just how dependent her course of study was on this particular book.

Forming relationships between music and the science of sound is important, but how do we hear the music? The human ear is a highly complex and sensitive instrument. It consists of a collection of tiny bones, tubes, and membranes that process the sounds we hear. The funnel-like shape of the outer ear collects sound waves and filters them through the ear passage, where they finally reach the eardrum and cause it to vibrate. These vibrations are converted into electrical signals by the inner ear and sent to the brain.

How do crickets, frogs, bats, and snakes hear? How do they make sounds? These are the sorts of questions that open the door to a large storehouse of ideas for a child. And you, as teacher, hold the key that unlocks the door. Learning about sound and hearing broadens the scope of music education even more.

The brain is another complex organ that plays an important role in our ability to hear and appreciate music. Its limbic system ignites when you listen to certain music. When you identify with a song (that you walked down the aisle to, for example) and tear up, you are relating emotionally to that piece. There are layers within the music that affect your emotions in general. Major chords sound happy; minor chords sound sad. Masters of music can control your emotions. (The music from *Psycho* can make you feel instantly frightened; the main theme from *Indiana Jones* can make you feel remarkably courageous.) If you watch *Psycho* when you are very young (which I don't recommend!) it will make you even more frightened than an adult would be because a child's brain is still growing and learning and forming attachments—the imagination is still so rich and the images it creates are so realistic that the child reacts more strongly to things (like music) that stimulate the imagination. This is why we need to guard our children against early exposure to things that are not good, true, or beautiful. And that includes music that is dishonoring, or frightening, too—all because the brain is such a fragile, delicate organ that is constantly forming new connections.

In his book, *This is Your Brain on Music*, Daniel Levitin explains that even among the elite, top-tier musicians, such as Arthur Rubenstein and Vladimir Horowitz, the emphasis is on technique, whereas a concertgoer's main concern is that he or she is emotionaly moved by the music. If technical prowess is of the utmost importance to the performer, how then is it that the listener's limbic system is ignited by the music? Does it happen accidentally, despite the fact that our best performers don't actually try to express any sort of emotion? Levitin asked the dean of one of the best music schools in North America if they ever teach emotional connectivity or expressiveness, and he said not particularly. Perhaps a top student might receive a few hours on the topic in a coaching session.

Diary entries from composers Beethoven and Tchaikovsky to B. B. King and Stevie Wonder all suggest that there is an emphasis on technical, mechanical factors, but that part of the emotional connectedness within their music remains a mystery. Stevie Wonder says he tries to get in the same frame of mind and heart he was in when he wrote a song when he performs it, but he has no idea how that makes the audience connect with it emotionally. It just does.

Neuroanatomist Andrew Arthur Abbie noted a connection in his 1934 research between movement, the brain, and music. His research is only now being proven true via ultrasound and other mechanisms of measurement. He believed the pathways from the brain stem and cerebellum to the frontal lobes could weave sensory experience and coordinated muscle movements into a "homogeneous fabric" and he says when that happens, it is the key to perfect expression in art.

A child's first listening experiences begin in utero with the rushing of blood, the beating of the human heart, and gurgles within the digestive system. Sound has been with us from the very beginning of our existence, but understanding it is a point of scientific inquiry. It will be taken on in starts and stops and bits and pieces throughout composer study, as we learn about this composer's technique of orchestration and that composer's mastery of chamber music. I mention it here where we are learning about the Science of Relations only to show you that there is no limit to how deep and wide a study you can offer a child when it comes to music. We experience it with our whole bodies, and it permeates our very souls.

INTANGIBLE RELATIONSHIPS: PATRONS ON DISPLAY

We have established that background knowledge can be crucial to helping a child understand a composer's work, but it is only a tool to open up to the child the fascinating world of musical knowledge. There are other, less tangible relations to be had. Ross King, in his book *Brunelleschi's Dome*, speaks of the Umiliati monks who came to Florence in the 1300s and brought with them a thriving wool industry. Soon, the best English wool was brought to be washed in the River Arno, dyed brilliant colors, and made into the finest cloth in all of Europe. Now that Florence was a wealthy city due to its expanded wool industry, says King, it needed a beautiful cathedral that exemplified its standing in the world of commerce. (It needed one? Must a city boast of its wealth and standing by building an impressive architectural structure? Does a city have to have an attitude or posture? Why would city rulers believe this necessary? To what lengths would they go in order to retain that standing?)

Florentine architects and artists spent two decades under Giotto creating a "280-foot campanile, with its bas-reliefs and incrustations of marble."[84] The Duomo took even longer to build. It was designed by Brunelleschi in 1420, but he worked on the project for twenty-seven years. Obviously, Florentine bankers believed in the importance of putting their wealth on exhibition, no matter the cost in time and money or risk to life and limb.

In studying the architecture of the time period, then, we need to also wrestle with its ideas—pride, power, prestige, boastfulness, authority, etc. There was more going on in Florence than simply a rebirth of classical ideas in art and architecture, science and inventions. Yes, the bustle of intellect was a wonderful thing after years where thought itself appeared to have become dark and stagnant. But beauty without cost or "art for art's sake" was seldom the goal in Renaissance Florence. Those who held the purse strings were in control, and they always had a reason for their artistic pursuits. There were exceptions. Leonardo da Vinci was quoted as saying, "I have offended God and mankind because my work did not reach the quality it should have."[85]

Motives and ideas—the intangibles in education—are important for the music student to understand, too. These are grand avenues within the house of mind that deserve to be explored alongside form, instrumentation, and history. Building relationship takes time and effort, and to fully relate to the composer whose music is the focus of a term of study involves taking the time to uncover the reasons for his or her success. These relations are harder to form and require complex critical thinking skills that will serve the student well later in life. Flexing these thinking muscles as early as developmentally possible will help students better understand human frailty, sin, guilt, self-deprecation, wisdom, foolishness, vanity, and a host of other intangible concepts.

Although it removes much of the romance we feel when listening to great music, when we dig into the history of a piece we may find that it was created solely for the purpose of keeping bread on the table. Some of the most beautiful music of the past was written because a duke wanted to impress a king or a wealthy patron wanted to give a performance that would garner him notoriety. The composer wrote about whatever the patron wanted. Often, the Catholic church or a particular pope commissioned the work.

Let's look for a moment at the efforts of the world's great composers. I'm thinking specifically now of the amount of time these great works took to complete. We know that Brunelleschi and Giotto spent years perfecting and creating architecture and art that would stand the test of time. How long did it take our best composers to complete their work? And at what cost?

Brunelleschi's health deteriorated while he was building the Duomo.

Michelangelo spent months high up on scaffolding painting the Sistine Chapel. It took Brahms twenty-one years to compose his first symphony. Beethoven worked on his fifth symphony for five years. Bach began his famous Mass in B Minor in 1724 and finished it shortly before his death in 1749. Going on those examples, one might say that taking extended periods of time will enable composers to produce their best work. Composers are notorious for their perfectionism, as are painters, authors, and others whose work is subjective. And yet, Rossini quickly jotted down his "Duet for Two Cats" late one evening when dueling cats in the alley outside his window were annoying him. And we still see it performed today!

Fame is often fleeting and flirtatious. A composer never knows what his or her public will respond to and what, after laborious years of steady effort, will be tossed by the wayside. In fact, many composers died without seeing fame or popularity of any sort and were buried in a pauper's grave. (Remember Vivaldi?) What distinguishes the work of someone like Vivaldi from another who, perhaps, remained lost to us forever? The goodness of God? The patronage of other composers or benefactors? History can be brutal, and the quest for fame can be an enormous wild-goose chase. I think we can safely say that any artistic endeavor is best performed to the glory of God and not in pursuit of fame or fortune. History may forget your contribution, but God never forgets. No matter how many years it takes to complete a work, God sees and rejoices in its creativity, finesse, the joy it brings its listeners—for the gift came from Him. I believe He enjoys watching us create. If I were the Creator of this massive, complex universe, I would enjoy watching human creativity unfold, too. It would feel like I feel on Christmas morning watching my children unwrap the marvelous gifts we so lovingly purchased for them.

Music, once admitted to the soul, becomes also a sort of spirit, and never dies.
—*Edward Bulwer-Lytton, Zanoni*

Chapter Ten

Narrating in Another Language:
The Pouring Forth of a Soul's Impressions

Music is the literature of the heart; it commences where speech ends.
                                              —*Alphonse de Lamartine*

Music is a language all its own. It enters through the ears but lands in the depths of the heart rather than being stored as knowledge or information in the annals of the mind. What a wondrous concept this is and at the same time, how puzzling to the human mind. And how daunting it is to teach a music lesson! It's in another language, after all. How can it be taught by a non-music-speaker? Must we first learn the language of music ourselves? How long will that take, and how proficient must we be before we are qualified to teach a composer study lesson? How can children narrate what they have not read? The questions fly into my mind as quickly as they fly into yours. I can see the inadequacy written across the new teacher's face. It's that deer-in-the-headlights look. "Help me! I don't understand music myself, so how can I teach it to my students?"

Music is heard, but it is also felt emotionally from a place deep within the human heart. Yes, we need to do some rudimentary music theory, study the life of the composer, learn a bit about instruments, and prepare ourselves for the lesson. I see the nervous tension beginning to rise. Don't worry. There is a schematic for this. You can learn a little of the necessary background knowledge beforehand (some of it can even be found in the appendices of this book). A little knowledge goes a long way; with a little knowledge the teacher can feel a bit more "adequate," if not completely confident. But now let's say we've come to the end of the lesson, and the child is supposed to narrate. Here is another difficulty. What should we require for a music study narration?

I believe narration must be thought out, planned for, and handled differently after a music lesson than it would be after a literature or even a picture study lesson. It is no longer a matter of "telling back" the story, because the story was not written on paper in English. It was written on our hearts by men of genius with musical notes. And every bit of it is important; every note matters. John Ruskin emphasizes this:

> Take any noble air, and you find, on examining it, that not one even of its faintest or shortest notes can be removed without destruction to the whole passage in which it occurs; and that every note in the passage is twenty times more beautiful so introduced than it would have been if played singly on the instrument. Precisely this degree of arrangement and relation must exist between every touch and line in a great picture. You must consider the whole as a prolonged musical composition.[86]

Here are a few tips:

1. Once your students have been prepared to listen to the piece (which should not be a long section, at least not at first), have them quiet themselves. They may need to close their eyes or lay their heads down on the desk or table in front of them.

2. Once every student is ready to listen and their hearts are prepared to take in the music, remind them of the background information you provided earlier—just a couple of tidbits to keep them focused: "Remember to listen for the quickening pace of the violins near the end of the piece" or "Don't forget this was written after the composer was told he had a fatal disease."

3. Play the excerpt.

4. Give the students a moment of silence to gather their thoughts.

5. Allow the students to respond to the music. If they have nothing to say, begin the narration process by asking open-ended questions: "How did

that opening section make you feel?" "What do you think was going through the composer's mind as he wrote that ending?" "Do you remember when this piece was written? If so, what do you think the composer was trying to say to his public when he wrote this?"

6. There is a story behind every piece of music. After the students finish narrating, you may want to give them a bit more information about the piece if their attention is still riveted on the music.

What next? Let's say you have listened to Beethoven's Moonlight Sonata. You have learned that he wrote it for a lost love. The students have narrated. Do you set that piece aside forever, never to listen to it again? In order for the piece to move from a child's short-term memory to the long-term memory where it can provide joy forever, you will need to play it repeatedly over the course of a few weeks and occasionally throughout the term. But do you need to provide a detailed composer study lesson each time? Not necessarily.

Once the first lesson has been completed, you have imprinted the piece on the students' young minds. The next time you play it for them, they may want to do a slow ballet-style dance around the room while listening. They may want to draw a picture of what they see in their minds while they listen to this particular piece. They may respond by writing a poem that matches the mood or tone of the music. The possibilities are endless, really. Each time they listen, they should respond in some way to the music, even if only to explain how it made them feel when they heard it at the end of a long day after playing outside as opposed to at the beginning of the day while seated calmly.

I recently read J. Paterson Smyth's recommendations for studying the book of Genesis from *The Bible for School and Home*.[87] He referenced an ancient Roman scholar who said teaching requires three things: *piacere, docere,* and *movere. Piacere* means "to interest" or "to please"—a great educator must first interest the student. According to Smyth, this takes careful planning and preparation before the lesson. A teacher who researches the topic in advance and plans out the lesson carefully will be at a great advantage compared to one who "wings it" and heads into the classroom without first digging deeply into the material for herself. In order to interest the student, you have to be interested yourself, at least interested enough to take some time to soak in the materials (in this case the music) in advance.

Docere means "to teach." Once you have interested your students in the music at hand by giving them tantalizing details about the life of the composer or the time period and culture, you play the music for them. If they have developed strong listening habits from early childhood (remember those days of listening to birds, crickets, the wind, etc.?) they will be up to the task of seeking out the instrumentation, emotion, dynamics, and other characteristics of each piece. You have taught them how to listen, and now they are listening.

Movere is perhaps the most important aspect of the lesson. It means "to move" or "to stir." You have interested the students in the lesson and given them the lesson; now you must move their hearts in some deeper way. This cannot be accomplished with preachiness or lecturing, however. So this is the most delicate point, the point at which you will either sink or swim. You have laid out a feast for their ears, and now they must reach for something deeper. They must respond with some living piece of themselves. If a lesson does not draw them toward God, provide living ideas, or otherwise move them to respond with their hearts, minds, or imaginations, something may be missing.

Not every piece of music will lead a student to beauty or truth or goodness or right living or joy. Sometimes, the lesson may be that debauchery leads to destruction or that the death of a loved one leaves behind a cavernous emptiness that can only be filled by God. But the motivation toward mental effort that comes from a lesson taught well, even if that means laying it before them and standing aside only to notice that they seem *not* to be responding, is worthwhile. In this last case, their response is indifference. But it *is* a response.

Each student's response to music will be different because every human being is unique. From the more concrete listener, you may hear "that first bit reminded me of the trash collector dropping the bin back down on the pavement of my street." From the more adept student of music, you may hear "that piece reminded me of the last day of camp when we got to row out to the center of the lake for a final prayer. The oars dipping into the water sound just like the repeating strings that ended the andante movement and our sadness at leaving camp is the same as those repeating flute bars at the beginning of the third movement." Every narration is valuable, and you may find that over time they become more and more detailed as the students advance in their music study.

Miss Mason trusted completely in Curwen's ideas, and I believe they hold merit for us even today. However, Mathilde Diez, a guest lecturer who wrote a *Parents' Review* article about music education, offers some other ideas that were considered refreshing in Miss Mason's time. In her article, called "Hints to Young Piano Teachers by a Foreigner,"[88] Diez mentions that parents tend to hire less experienced or less qualified teachers when their children are young and move on to more qualified teachers for advanced music study. She thinks care should be taken to hire the very best teachers early on so that bad habits don't become ingrained and hinder the student's ability to thrive later on when the music becomes more difficult. I agree with her, although in my experience the best music teachers often take only advanced pupils. Still, I believe the same care we are taking to teach our children about music through composer study and listening lessons, using methods we know work and preparing each lesson in advance, ought to apply to the teaching of music practice—that is, the applied skills of singing and playing instruments.

Before we leave the topic of narration, let's think about learning styles for a moment. When our family listened to the music of Prokofiev, our children fell in love with—no, not *Peter and the Wolf*—*Romeo and Juliet*. We purchased tickets to the Virginia Symphony's student performance and ordered a recording and study guide package to prepare for the concert. Our children were young, and we wanted them to connect with the music. It was an impressive package filled with interesting stories about the composers. I am so thankful for the Virginia Symphony's careful pre-planning. We listened to the recording in the car for a few weeks, and the children learned the basic melodies. We arrived on the day of the concert filled with anticipation, and we were not disappointed. But we did notice that other students in attendance who were not quite so prepared seemed restless and bored.

As we listened to the music at home, I noticed that each of my children was responding differently. Our eldest daughter had created a film version of the story in her mind, focusing on characters from her then-favorite movie, Disney's *A Bug's Life*. Our younger daughter had created plot lines from Brian Jacques' *Redwall* series, using Prokofiev's "Montagues and Capulets" as background music. All four of our children dramatically brought to life the story of Jezebel from the Bible, complete with her entrails being eaten by dogs (they placed a dog biscuit beneath my daughter's shirt and called in our bichon frise to nibble at it for emphasis), also to the music of Prokofiev's *Romeo and Juliet.* All this drama and imaginary play came from their interest in the dramatic flair of Prokofiev's *Romeo and Juliet.* But what visual learners took away from the music would not be the same as what auditory learners might get out of it. A left-brained child who is more analytical than imaginative might notice the changing rhythms or marvel at the intricacy of the design. A philosophical student might wonder if Prokofiev was trying to make a political statement. A kinesthetic learner might not be concerned with the story at all, but would still thoroughly enjoy the music as a backdrop for a larger-than-life sword fight with his brother.

Although it's important to strengthen weaker areas, there is no right or wrong narration, in my opinion, at least when it comes to responding to music. As the years progress and a child's store of knowledge increases (dare I suggest there is such a storehouse within a human being when we're fighting the idea that we are receptacles of knowledge?), composer study narrations will gradually increase in complexity. As dexterity of musical ability increases, so will the level of detail within their narrations. If you are not seeing this, go back and look over your preparation lesson and see if maybe you have missed the "interest" stage, the *piacere.* It's never too late to fix a glitch in method. The results will be worth the effort.

Now for something you may find a bit difficult. In the appendix to Glover's book *The Term's Music* are "specimen examination questions" that provide examples of what Miss Mason's students were expected to know about music. I think it's important for us to reach for higher ground while educating our children, and I am the first to admit that I've lost my footing along the way many times. Please don't be overwhelmed by these exam questions, but do read through them and see what Miss Mason's students were able to do. It's not impossible to believe that one day our students might accomplish this level of music analysis and create the same depth of relationship with the music they listen to or with the books they are reading. I believe if we take seriously the admonitions in Chapter Three as we are growing avid listeners, learning about instrumentation and form, and identifying with various composers, their time periods, homelands, and personhoods, this type of work may be possible by the time our students reach Form IV.

SPECIMEN EXAMINATION QUESTIONS

FIRST YEAR:

1ST TERM (HANDEL)

1. Contrast the methods of Handel and J. S. Bach with special reference to their respective treatment of Variations.

2. Justify the assertion that Handel was as representative of his age as J. S. Bach was unrepresentative.

3. Relate the incidents resulting in the composition of the "Water Music."

4. Write a few lines on each of the following: Canons; Lesson; Buononcini; Serse; The Messiah; The Harmonious Blacksmith; Doubles.

2ND TERM (BACH)

1. Write a short account of the meeting between Frederick the Great and Bach.

2. Describe the contest between Bach and Marchand.

3. Contrast the respective environments in which Bach and Handel were working at the end of their lives.

4. Write a few lines on each of the following: Harpsichord; Silbermann pianofortes; The Well-Tempered Klavier; Anna Magdalena; The Musical Offering; Motett; Capriccio on the departure of a beloved brother.

3RD TERM (MOZART)

1. Relate the incidents which led to the composition of the Requiem Mass.

2. Describe briefly the events connected with Mozart's visit to London.

3. Estimate the importance of the romantic element in Mozart's music.

4. Write a few lines on each of the following: J. C. Bach; sonata form; The *Marriage of Figaro*; rondo; Nannerl; G minor symphony; Archbishop of Salzburg.

SECOND YEAR:

1ST TERM (BEETHOVEN)

1. Into how many periods is Beethoven's life divided? State a few characteristics of each period.

2. Give the context of the following: La Malinconia; mehr Ausdruck der Empfindung als Malerey (more expression of feeling than painting); Cavatina; Hammerklavier; Sonata quasi una fantasia.

3. What part did Beethoven play in the evolution of the concerto? Contrast his methods with those employed in the "concerto grosso" of Handel's day.

4. Write a few lines on each of the following: Count Rasoumovsky; Choral Symphony; Albrechtsberger; Bagatelles; Sonata Pathetique; The Beethoven Rondo; the Kreutzer sonata; scherzo.

2ND TERM (SCHUBERT)

1. What is the characteristic weakness of style in Schubert's large scale works? Illustrate with special reference to the Pianoforte Sonata in B flat.

2. What are the essential differences between the "Lied" or art song of Schubert and the folk song or ballad?

3. Give three instances in Schubert's music of the employment of themes of one composition in another wholly unrelated work.

4. Write a few lines on each of the following: The Erlking; The cardinal virtues of good song writing; Rosamunde; Salieri; discovery of the C major symphony in 1838; Schone Mullerin; the Convict.

3RD TERM (SCHUMANN)

1. How many kinds of Children's Music are there: Give examples of each type. In what category would you place Schumann's "Scenes of Childhood" and why?

2. Write a short account of Schumann's activities as a critic and journalist.

3. In what way did the Romantic movement influence the form of musical compositions?

4. Write a few lines on each of the following: Clara Wieck; Traumerci; Genoveva; Florestan; G.A.D.E.; Jean Paul Richter; Schumann's use of the "Marseillaise."

Third Year:

1st Term (Brahms)

1. Write a short account of the Brahms-Wagner controversy.

2. Relate some of the incidents connected with the intimacy of Brahms with the Schumann family.

3. Write a note on Brahms' methods of instrumentation.

4. Write a few lines on each of the following: Joseph Joachim; Johann Strauss the younger; the Sonatensatz; Marxsen; the two versions of the waltzes; Brahms' treatment of German folksong; Remenyi.

2nd TERM (Wagner)

1. Write a brief account of Wagner's theory of music drama, and contrast his methods with those of his predecessors.

2. Trace the gradual evolution of the leitmotif in Wagner's later operas and music dramas.

3. Give a short historical outline of the composition of the poems and music of the "Ring" dramas, and account for the several redundancies therein.

4. Write a few lines on each of the following: The Tarnelm; Montsalvat; Bayreuth; "Wittemberg Nightingale," Villa Triebschen; valve horns; "Siegfried Idyll," Meyerbeer.

3rd Term (Grieg)

1. Give an account of the meeting between Grieg and Liszt.

2. Enumerate shortly any mannerisms, which you may have observed in Grieg's music.

3. Estimate shortly the effect of nationalism in music generally, stating whether you consider it beneficial or detrimental.

4. Write a few lines on each of the following: Ole Bull; Vinje; Troldhaugen; Peer Gynt; Alexander Grieg; Ludwig Holberg; Niels Gade.

FOURTH YEAR:

1ST TERM (MOUSSORGSKY AND BORODIN)

1. Write a short account of the work of the Russian "five" and estimate shortly their significance in the history of music.

2. Contrast the work of Moussorgsky and Borodin with special reference to the music studied this term.

3. Estimate the importance of the realistic factor in Moussorgsky's music. What is meant by the term "programme-music?"

4. Write a few lines on each of the following: Prince Igor; Dargomijsky; Byldo; Pushkin; Russian folksong; Mazurka; Hartmann; Khovantchina.

2ND TERM (DVOŘÁK)

1. What are the main characteristics of Czech folk music and how are they exemplified in Dvorak's music?

2. Detail the compositions which Dvorak wrote under the stimulus of Negro [vernacular of the time period] folk music and recount the circumstances in which he became the subject to its influence.

3. Mention a few of the most striking characteristics of Dvorak's style of composition.

4. Write a few lines on each of the following: Bagatellen; motto theme; Scotch snap; the Spectre Bride; Furiant; Humoreske; Smetana; Dumka.

3RD TERM (DEBUSSY)

1. What is meant by the whole tone scale: Write out the whole tone scale beginning on C sharp.

2. What is the Dorian mode? Give an example from the music in the syllabus of its employment by Debussy.

3. Trace the affinity between Debussy and the French Clavecin composers of the eighteenth century.

4. Write a few lines on each of the following: Bergamasque; l'Enfant Prodigue; St. Germain-en-Laye; overtones; Prix de Rome; Debussy and Boris Godounov; Jimbo's Lullaby.[89]

That wasn't so hard, was it? It was? Yes, I know, it was for me, too, when I first read it. I was extremely discouraged. I think at the start of my journey with my own children I brought a childlike love for classical music into our family, and I am happy about that. It was effortless and became part of who we were. Looking back, I do see areas of lack, however—areas that I did not even realize I was supposed to include. I was comforted by the words of E. T. Campagnac, who wrote a beautiful introduction to *The Enjoyment of Music*—a book by A. W. Pollitt that appeared on Miss Mason's syllabus for Forms V and VI for high school:

> Dr Pollitt tells us that we must habituate ourselves to the atmosphere of great music. For this purpose we must go often and stay long in the region of that atmosphere. We cannot quickly and hurriedly achieve familiarity with greatness.

So we need to take composer study seriously and give it due time in the course of our days. We must slowly savor it, too. Miss Mason included official composer study only once a week, but that was strictly the study of the composer for the term. Music itself was another matter entirely and required daily practice and study. Campagnac continues:

> Majesty is robed; but the robes do not make majesty. Yet the dress, the sound, may properly attract the eye and hold the ear of those who are still unable to perceive that the dress at once shields and embellishes a living spirit, or that the sound it expresses gives protection to ideas.

Now I'm beginning to understand why Miss Mason chose this book for her students. The ideas! We are learning to absorb living ideas from music, but it doesn't happen overnight. At first, we just enjoy the pretty clothes that enrobe it, but one day we will journey deeper and find its ideas. And it will become increasingly important as we journey forward to remember to ask our students to narrate back for us the ideas behind the music and not simply the musical form or fashion.

Campagnac finishes by saying:

> Education is never complete . . . The nearer we are brought to the goal, the clearer the certainty with which we apprehend the ideas which in many forms of beauty we have been learning to revere.[90]

This is why we must never get discouraged. If we do our job right and employ the methods Miss Mason left us, our children will continue to learn and grow and invest in ideas and enjoy beauty and goodness throughout their lives.

No neat system is of any use; it is the very nature of a system to grow stale in the using; every subject, every division of a subject, every lesson, in fact, must be brought up for examination before it is offered to the child as to whether it is living, vital, of a nature to invite the living Intellect of the universe.

—Charlotte Mason, Parents and Children

Chapter Eleven

Solfège and Tonic Sol-Fa:
A Uniform Language for Sight-Singing

Music expresses that which cannot be said and on which it is impossible to be silent.

—*Victor Hugo*

Writing about solfège is problematic. Simply put, it is a system of note names—do, re mi, and so on—used to express the different pitches in the musical scale. Over the years, people have developed several ways to express solfège with sign language and written notation. Without meeting you face to face and showing you the various hand signals and shape notes that constitute a complete understanding of this sight-singing method, it's difficult to translate on paper. Fortunately, there are many websites and even a few YouTube videos that illustrate the use of solfège and can help you understand.

The most important aspect of solfège, to me, is that it is universal. Imagine, for a moment, that you are sitting in a choir rehearsal in a small village in India. The language is unfamiliar to you. The alphabet is unfamiliar, too. How, then, might you sight-sing a piece using the traditional English note names for something as simple as a C major scale: C, D, E, F, G, A, B, C? What Hindi characters correspond to the English alphabet letters? You see the problem.

Solfège gives every human being a universal way to speak to one another through music, and even a way to speak to the world together in unison. It's a marvelous concept, really. The shape of each note tells you where it falls on the scale, and the hand signals and syllables (do, re, mi, fa, sol, la, ti, do) are the same in every language. Voila! You can now sight-sing anywhere on the planet with an equal chance of understanding and communicating through music.

Miss Mason recommended the use of solfège, so we include it in our music studies. But I want you to understand her reasons. In *Home Education* she praises the "admirable educational effects of the Tonic Sol-fa Method." (Tonic sol-fa was a sight-singing system based on solfège that was popular at the time.) Miss Mason writes:

> Children learn by it in a magical way to produce sign for sound and sound for sign, that is, they can not only read music, but can write the notes for, or make the proper hand signs for, the notes of a passage sung to them. Ear and Voice are simultaneously and equally cultivated.[91]

Barbara Davenport wrote several articles about music for *The Parents' Review*, and she recommended playing listening games:

> The cultivation of a good ear is perhaps the most important thing in all music, whether pianoforte or any other instrument. A splendid way to cultivate the ear in childhood—a way that is sure to amuse, so strongly does it resemble the magic of a "game,"—is to send the child away from the piano whilst you strike single notes one after the other, making it guess each time what note you are playing. Very soon an intelligent pupil gets used to recognising the different notes; begins to be able to judge distances of tone, semitone, major and minor thirds, and so on; and the exercise of ear becomes the greatest delight.[92]

Miss Mason believed the child's "knowledge of the theory of music and his ear training [should] keep pace with his power of execution."[93] This short examination of music study, tucked neatly into *Home Education* on page 315, is one of the few places where Miss Mason addresses music study. Elsewhere, she chooses primarily to entrust the topic to Curwen, whom she believed had a much stronger understanding of music pedagogy. I gleaned this from reading about how Miss Mason first came to include music study in her programmes. This was the one area she did not appear to understand well. She added this subject later after hearing from Mrs. Howard Glover that placing young children in touch with great music could be a positive learning experience and might open the door a bit wider to the feast at large. Glover spoke about the origins of Miss Mason's views on Music(al) Appreciation at the Ambleside Conference of the Parents' Union in 1922:

> Musical Appreciation—which is so much before the eye at the present moment—originated in the P.N.E.U. about twenty-five years ago. At that time I was playing to my little child much of the best music in which I was interested, and Miss Mason happened to hear of what I was doing. She realised that music might give great joy and interest to the life of all, and she felt that just as children in the P.U.S. were given the greatest literature and art, so they should have the greatest music as well.[94]

While she did not have a strong grasp on music pedagogy, I believe Miss Mason was a robust singer and a great poet (read some of her original work and you will, too). She appears to have thoroughly enjoyed music—the singing of hymns, her beloved orchestral and chamber music, folk songs that unite a culture. But she left the "how" of teaching it to Curwen. To understand the origins of tonic sol-fa, then—the method Miss Mason praised so highly—we need to take a peek at how Curwen's father-in-law came up with the idea for this method of teaching children to sight-read music.

To begin, we should recognize the contributions of Sarah Glover (no relation to Mrs. Howard Glover as far as I can tell), who was a contemporary of Reverend John Curwen's and who came up with the original idea for sight-singing using tonic sol-fa with hand signals. John Curwen borrowed extensively from Glover's ideas to form his own version of the method. He was commissioned at a conference of Sunday-school teachers to come up with a simple way to teach music for use in Sunday-school singing. He researched several methods and decided to modify Glover's to form what is now known as the Curwen method of tonic sol-fa. Another sight-singing method, the Kodály method, is perhaps better known in our time, but to honor Miss Mason's ideas, we will stick with Curwen's here.

Curwen's basic thought in developing the method was that singers do not need to know what key a piece is written in in order to sight-read it. Regular staff notation is necessary for pianists and other instrumentalists, but a singer needs only a starting note to begin singing a song in any key at all. Thus, it's possible to trick an entire choir into believing they are singing in one key when they are really singing in another. This is helpful because sometimes a piece of music is written in a key that is too high for singers. Using tonic sol-fa eliminates the necessity of transposing each part for the choir. They will simply begin on a different note. Singers read music by intervals, not specific sounds.

In his book, Curwen goes beyond merely explaining what tonic sol-fa is. He also offers tips on how to teach it:

> In the first place, we teach singing without the help of an instrument. This is in order to give the learner independence. . . . Tonic Sol-fa singers are trained to strike their notes by the unaided judgment of their ears. This judgment is formed upon the place which each sound holds in the key, and not upon its absolute pitch or the number of semitones by which it is separated from the last note. Singers are taught to recognize a characteristic effect in each of the tones of the scale, called its mental effect.[95]

I learned sight-singing in a similar way. Since I grew up in Texas, I learned the interval of a fourth, from C in a C major scale to F, by remembering "The Eyes of Texas are Upon You." The Eyes is the phrase that is the distance of a fourth. If you don't know the song, you can create your own. The first two notes of Amazing Grace is a common example. The distance of a major third, from C to E, is the sound of a doorbell ringing. These devices help children sight-sing when the music is unfamiliar. But the added assistance tonic sol-fa offers is that each note has a name. They learn, then, that the sound of mi-do is the sound of a doorbell.

Chords are used to teach the scale in tonic sol-fa. Curwen explains:

> We lay stress on the habit of teaching the scale gradually by means of

the consonant chords which it contains. Consonance is more natural to the untrained ear than dissonance; and pure intonation is better taught by striking the tones of a chord in succession than by running up or down the scale, whose adjacent notes are dissonant with each other. First, the learner has to be made familiar with the tonic chord, doh, me, soh, and has to sound its tones at the will of the teacher; next he does the same with the dominant chord (soh, te, ray); and lastly, with the subdominant (fah, lah, doh). This completes the seven sounds. After this, he is confined to tunes and exercises which contain no more than these seven tones, and do not change the key.[96]

Next, Curwen teaches children meter and rhythm (divisions of time) using a French method devised by M. Paris. This is similar to the one-ee-and-uh, two-ee-and-uh that so many choir directors use today:

The pupil is taught to sing his early exercises on one tone to the Time Names. Thus he first learns the Time and then the tune of a piece. This may be considered a needless hair-splitting, but for beginners it is not so.

Curwen says the teacher considers the ears and voices of the students the material. The teacher begins without any signs at all and only introduces them gradually as needed. He borrowed these ideas from Pestalozzi, who was an educationalist Charlotte Mason was familiar with. Curwen's final words on tonic sol-fa are these: "let the easy come before the difficult; introduce the real and concrete before the ideal and abstract; teach the elemental before the compound; and do one thing at a time."

Curwen moved on from these basic ideas to methods of teaching harmony, minor keys, and more. You can find further information on tonic sol-fa methodology and practice exercises in his book, *The Standard Course of Lessons on the Tonic Sol-fa Method of Teaching to Sing*.[97]

One historian explains the method this way (please don't be alarmed at the complex explanation. We do not necessarily need to use this exact notation in order to find success using sol-fa in our schools and homeschools):

Curwen made several modifications to Glover's sol-fa notation and finally decided upon a pitch representation system which utilized the first letter (in lower case) of each of the solmization tones (doh, ray, me, fah, soh, lah, te) and a rhythmic notation system which utilized bar lines, half bar lines and semicolons prefixing strong beats, medium beats and weak beats respectively in each measure. For marking the subdivisions of beats he used a full stop for half divisions and a comma for quarter divisions, and for continuation of a tone from one beat to the next he employed a dash.[98]

For sharps and flats, the syllables are changed to "e" for sharps Standard Course")and "a" (ah) for flats (e.g. "fe" and "rah" instead of "fah" and "ray"). So there is a syllable for every chromatic note in the scale, and any melody can be written without resorting to regular staff notation. The entire process was ingenious, and it worked very well for young children during Miss Mason's time.

Curwen and his son eventually founded a popular sheet music company, and they had unfettered access to schools across England. By 1872, he was able to print editions of *The Standard Course* that excluded regular staff notation altogether in favor of his own notation system. He printed vocal music, textbooks, and instrumental music using solely sol-fa notation.

Predictably, I suppose, using tonic sol-fa notation alone led to his downfall. Curwen spread his educational method as far abroad as Australia, New Zealand, South Africa, Canada, the United States, India, Madagascar, China, Japan, and the South Sea Islands, but it fell from popularity once he removed all regular staff notation. I can't help wondering what might have happened had he not altered the way he printed his music. Perhaps we might all have learned to sing using tonic sol-fa. After all, by 1891, 2.5 million children were using this method in their official elementary school studies. You could even get certified as a sol-fa educator at his Tonic Sol-fa College, later renamed Curwen Memorial College and now The Curwen Institute, a branch of the John Curwen Society.[99]

MANUAL SIGNS FOR THE TONES OF THE SCALE
(From Curwen's "Standard Course")

DOH

RAY

ME

FAH

SOH

LAH

TI

DOH

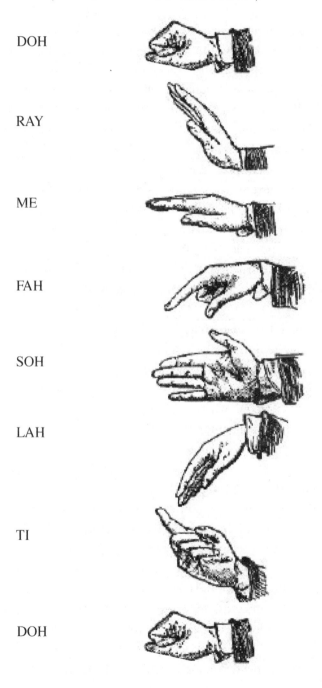

MUSIC DICTATION

There is one topic we've yet to discuss—one aspect of a Charlotte Mason education, so to speak—and that is dictation. I did not find any evidence that Miss Mason's students did music dictation. But does that mean that music dictation has no place in a Charlotte Mason education today? An article posted by the Philharmonia Orchestra in the UK says that "dictation is one of the most difficult elements of aural tests, but also one of the most useful—it's fantastic to be able to listen to a melody and write it down."[100]

Suppose a student proved to be particularly gifted at music. Would not dictation be an important door to open in the House of Mind, one we want to make sure to open up to all since we cannot know who will exhibit a natural giftedness and who might rise to it with eagerness given the opportunity? With practice, it's quite possible that one day your student may be able to sit down with staff paper and write music from memory.

My guitar teacher, Milo Deering (whom I just discovered nearly forty years later has been touring with Don Henley of the Eagles), once asked me if there was a song I'd like to learn to play on the guitar. I mentioned three or four recent pop songs, and he quickly jotted down the melodies and harmonies for me, with the understanding of where a teenaged girl's fingers could and could not reach on the frets of a guitar. For this, he had to know the fingerboard as well as a pianist knows where every note falls on a piano; he had to know notation; he had to understand how to notate rhythm changes, create uniform measures, write down the dynamics. The list goes on. A human being's mind is capable of all of this, given practice in the skill of listening and notation. Early work with music dictation could really benefit our students.

The Philharmonia Orchestra's article offers several practical steps for implementing dictation. Begin by listening to the rhythm and writing it above the staff to refer to as you jot down the melody. Next work on the notes themselves. You can hum them quietly to yourself, finding places where the melody repeats. Break down the piece into sections, and bit by bit, write them down. At first, of course, you may listen as many times as necessary. Later, as you become more adept at dictation, you may be able to listen once and write it down. (Or maybe not. It seems like quite a tall order to me!)

I would recommend reading the full article as long as it's still online. It includes a few simple exercises for students new to dictation. Go ahead and give it a try. You may find you have one of the next great composers sitting beside you.

True genius without heart is a thing of nought—for not great understanding alone, not intelligence alone, nor both together, make genius. Love! Love! Love! that is the soul of genius.

—Nikolaus Joseph von Jacquin, from an entry in Mozart's souvenir album

Chapter Twelve

Opera:
Embracing Glory and Passion in Music

One can't judge Wagner's opera Lohengrin after a first hearing, and I certainly don't intend to hear it a second time.

—*Gioachino Rossini*

My love affair with opera began when I was about eight years old. My parents were Dallas Symphony musicians, and they were part of the pit orchestra for the Dallas Opera's performance of *Samson et Dalila* by Saint-Saëns. Either my parents didn't believe in babysitters, didn't want to pay babysitters, or maybe they just liked having me around. They took me with them to many rehearsals over the years, but this time I was at an opera performance, seated on a backstage stool, when my dad took me by the hand and said, "Come with me."

It was intermission. He walked me across the stage and down the steps to the velvet seats in the music hall at Fair Park. I can still remember the echo of my clicking heels on the wooden stage. I self-consciously tried to make myself as small as possible and my steps as quiet as I could, but no one would have noticed if I hadn't. My father said, "I spotted some empty seats, and it's so late now that I know they'll stay empty." I sat down and smoothed my fingers across the soft, maroon-colored velvet. The chair rocked gently as I swung my legs. The lights dimmed. The orchestra tuned. The opera singers took the stage.

I don't remember much more about that night. All other memories fled during the final scene in which Samson cries out with a loud voice, sings his heart out, and shoves the pillars until the entire set falls to the ground with an enormous crash. I shivered as his powerful voice filled the music hall. Tears gathered in the corners of my eyes. It was an incredible moment.

That was the night I fell in love with opera.

I know it's silly, but I just watched *Samson et Dalila* again online and cried. Again. After all these years. That's the power opera has to move you. And as Opera Carolina director James Meena says, "There is more to opera than just the music." The plot, the rising action and climax of an almost always tragic tale of woe, the set design, costumes, makeup, wigs, blocking, acting, and orchestration all come together to move the audience. Unlike orchestral music or even an oratorio, opera has the added ability to transport the viewer/listener to another time and place, to drop us into the story and leave us there, spellbound by the crescendos, the powerful voices, the impassioned pleas from a doomed protagonist.

After that first experience watching *Samson et Dalila*, my heart was torn. It was diseased. Infected. Crushed. It pulsed with passion. I was afflicted with a malady that defied all eight-year-old logic. I was magically, completely, wholeheartedly in love with opera. And the disease was about to spread. I could not get enough of this powerful music. And that was a problem, because the symphony did not perform for every opera. My parents took on pit orchestra work on the side, and they often chose not to say yes to it. I begged and was permitted to see I *Pagliacci*. I loved it. *La Bohème* I loved even more.

Years later, longing for some deeper music study for my children, I enrolled them in the Choir School at St. Peter's Episcopal Church in Charlotte, NC. It was a tough program! They had to study hard each year to earn ribbons and progress through levels of music theory and its application. Not only that, they were required to learn solfège, to my great delight. Their teacher, Carol Lillard, was patient and kind but firm. And they learned. And grew.

Then it happened.

The choir director was asked if his children's touring choirs might participate in an Opera Carolina performance of *Tosca* by Puccini. He said yes and off the children went to be fitted with wigs, costumes, and shoes. They rehearsed for what seemed like hours each day until they knew their piece backwards and forwards. It was called "Te Deum." Opera Carolina imported lavish sets from Italy—giant pieces that were veritable works of art. The children were awestruck. They had never performed in a professional opera, much less in full costume with such gorgeous scenery.

We did not fully realize the impact this experience was going to have on our children's love of opera and orchestral music—although I did have my suspicions when I caught my little "choirboy" Hannah crouching in the hallway beneath the speaker while the other kids were in the green room playing cards. She was listening to the soprano sing "Vissi d'arte," with tears streaming down her cheeks.

Fast forward ten years, and I was privileged to watch our Hannah graduate from Berklee College of Music with a Vocal Performance and Film Scoring degree. She became the president of Berklee's opera club, staged *The Pirates of Penzance, Hansel and Gretel,* and more. She went on to earn a lead role with Opera Carolina's touring opera right after she graduated.

I can't emphasize enough the beauty and connection a child receives by performing music rather than only watching it or listening to recordings. I hope you'll try getting your students into a choir program or volunteering to be a supernumerary (like a movie extra but in an opera) with a local opera company. The opportunities may be sparse if you live in a rural area, but try a local church choir or community choir.

Participating in operas, taking voice lessons, singing arias, and developing relationships with your local opera company, or even with a company further away if you live in a small town or rural area, can be invaluable to your music appreciation experience. Our family got to know Maestro James Meena here in North Carolina through talks he gave before and after each opera performance. We developed a relationship with him. A friendship. Then, to our great surprise, we discovered we had a mutual friend and ran into him at a party. What a treat that was. You'd be amazed at how open professional musicians can be to interacting with children who show an interest in their work. We are raising the next generation of classical music lovers, and that interests them greatly.

Over the years, our children have performed in *La Bohème, Pearl Fishers, Tales of Hoffman, Marriage of Figaro, Turandot, Fidelio,* and *Carmen.* I've undoubtedly left out a few—I hope they'll forgive me. I remember once driving Hilary through blizzard conditions to get her uptown for a sparsely attended performance of *La Bohème*. Those who did manage to make it to the auditorium through the storm were avid opera-goers and applauded vigorously at the brilliant performance, even though some chorus members had been snowbound and unable to perform as planned.

During their *Pearl Fishers* rehearsals and performances, our children asked permission to create a documentary, using an old video camera. They interviewed the performers, the dancers, the chorus members. They shot scenes of the dancers, talked about the building and sets, and interviewed Maestro Meena. They got some great video of the tenor and baritone duet "Au fond du temple saint." What an incredible learning experience that was.

Their love was deepening. Crescendoing. It was beautiful to behold as a Charlotte Mason educator, as a parent, and as the daughter of symphony musicians. My parents have both passed away, so I feel a tender whisper of delight brush over me each time one of our children performs in an opera, an orchestra, or any musical performance. Something familiar, like a favorite quilt, wraps me in its warmth and carries me back to a time when they were still here with us, creating a house filled with music for me.

There is a deep vein of pure gold hidden within each child, a special giftedness. Every child has the potential to love and enjoy music. The opportunities are endless, and it all began for me with *Samson et Dalila* in a darkened auditorium filled with a hushed audience in Dallas. The power of music. To jar us. To wound us. To thrill us. To heal us. I believe there will be glorious music in Heaven, and I know the foretaste we've been given here on earth is only a tiny glimpse of the glory to come. And you never know what beautiful experiences are right around the next bend in the road until you take that first step.

Massenet feels it as a Frenchman, with powder and minuets. I shall feel it as an Italian, with desperate passion.

—*Giacomo Puccini*

Chapter Thirteen

Soul-Stirring Melodies:
Folk Song Study

All music is folk music. I ain't never heard a horse sing a song.
—Louis Armstrong

We know Miss Mason spoke about the importance of learning folk songs, but I'd like to bring the essence of her method into the twenty-first century as we look at her educational plan. A friend who has studied folk songs at length for many years recently told me Miss Mason included them in her programmes because it was customary for schools of her era to include folk songs in their curriculum. But this would be a departure from her usual revolutionary thinking. To me, simply doing something because it's what everyone was doing in schools at the time runs contrary to her careful, studied methodology. *Why would she do that?* I asked myself. Maybe because she saw that it was one of the many currents of educational thought that was actually working? Because it gave the students a sense of national identity and a sense of cultural belonging? I decided to take a look at the musical culture of Miss Mason's England to find out more.

Ballads, brass bands, and parlor music were the rage in England during Miss Mason's time period, though English folk music had come to the Isles with the Anglo-Saxons and Caedmon reported that Medieval musicians sang "vain and idle songs" through oral tradition long before they had sheet music

on which to write it down.[101] Parlor music would have included everything
from Thomas Moore's *Irish Melodies* to Italian opera, patriotic songs, excerpts
from blackface minstrel shows (unfortunately), and religious songs.

After parlor music came outings to music halls and dance bands. The wide
availability of sheet music in the nineteenth century led to a rise in what can
only be called "popular music." Yes, pop music, with a simple beat, a catchy
melody, and a repeated chorus. Traditional folk songs were being replaced at
the turn of the twentieth century—by pop music. Could this be why Miss
Mason so strongly urged us to keep folk songs in our educational plan? So that
we would not lose our cultural heritage to whatever the latest whim or flight of
fancy might be?

HISTORICAL PERSPECTIVE

While Renaissance madrigals were performed with accompanying
bagpipes, hurdy-gurdies, and fiddles, the earliest folk music would have been
sung a capella. These were lusty pub songs of lost love and damsels in distress.
They were sappy and poetic and romantic. One you may have heard of is
"Scarborough Faire," made popular by Simon and Garfunkel back in the
1970s. These pub songs are not the nursery songs we typically think of when
we begin learning folk songs in our Charlotte Mason schools and homeschools
(although our daughter did learn a few when she was studying fiddle tunes).
Some of them take a little explaining, like "What Do You Do with a Drunken
Sailor?" or "The Lusty Young Smith," but these are easily avoided or can be
used as morality tales. And we have many others to choose from.

Folk songs and sea shanties were for adults, but children would have learned
lullabies and rhyming songs for the nursery. Miss Mason recommended two
books for the task of teaching early folk songs: *The Baby's Opera* and *The Baby's
Bouquet*, both by Walter Crane. These beautifully illustrated and decorated
songbooks contained sheet music and extra verses. Some of the songs might be
familiar to you already.

The Baby's Opera included:
  The Mulberry Bush
  Oranges and Lemons
  Lavender's Blue
  I Saw Three Ships
  Ding Dong Bell
  Three Blind Mice
  Dickory Dock
  Song of Sixpense
  Hush-a-bye Baby

The Baby's Bouquet included:
  Polly Put the Kettle On
  Hot Cross Buns
  The Little Woman and the Peddler
  Lucy Locket
  If All the World Were Paper
  The North Wind and the Robin
  Aiken Drum
  London Bridge
  Looby Light

We also have a rich heritage of nursery songs in America, songs that give our children a common heritage in much the same way nursery rhymes do. Here are a few of the songs of childhood that are known and loved in America:

  A Sailor Went to Sea
  The Ants Go Marching
  Apples and Bananas
  Baby Beluga
  The Bear Went Over the Mountain
  BINGO
  Boom, Boom, Ain't It Great to Be Crazy
  Buffalo Gals
  Do Your Ears Hang Low

Down by the Bay
Down on Grandpa's Farm
Father Abraham
Down in the Valley
Five Little Monkeys
The Gingerbread Man
Green Grass Grew All Around
Head and Shoulders, Knees and Toes
I've Been Working on the Railroad
Home on the Range
If You're Happy and You Know It
John Jacob Jingleheimer Schmidt
Kumbayah
Michael Finnegan
The More We Get Together
My Bonnie Lies Over the Ocean
The Noble Duke of York
Old Joe Clark
Old Macdonald Had a Farm
Row, Row, Row Your Boat
Shoo Fly, Don't Bother Me
Skip to My Lou
This Land Is Your Land
This Old Man
The Wheels on the Bus
When Johnny Comes Marching Home
When the Saints Go Marching In
Yankee Doodle
You Are My Sunshine

Did you recognize most of the titles above? I knew all of them because when I was a child we learned them in school. What are our techno-genius children learning at school in our fast-paced, postmodern society? Are we preserving our heritage of folk songs and nursery rhymes for our children? Our children's children? Is music even a priority for young children anymore?

If we don't ensure that these songs remain in our national vocabulary, chances are they will be lost to us forever, and while losing "Baby Beluga" is not going to keep me up at night, losing "This Land Is Your Land" just might.

Despite my initial inclination to look only at British history, my next stop was the Library of Congress's archive of "work, school, and leisure activities in America from 1894-1915." What a treasure trove of remarkable photos, film clips, and papers are accessible to us online! While I was looking for information about folk music, I found some long-forgotten ragtime sheet music appropriate to our cause (e.g., *Grace and Beauty: A Classy Rag*). I was startled to discover that ragtime music was not entirely meant for entertainment purposes. Some of it was written to inspire people in much the same way folk songs do. They helped the poor carry on despite adversity and enlivened the souls of the listeners. With this in common with folk music, I became intrigued. From the introduction to the sheet music for "*Cole Smoak* Rag":

The writer believes in very truth that *Cole Smoak* is a positive inspiration. Human language is not equal to the task of painting the interior thoughts of the soul. It is also certain that all souls do not slack their thirst from the same fountain. *Cole Smoak* appeals to the writer in language unutterable.[102]

Scott Joplin wrote *The Chrysanthemum Rag* after reading *Alice in Wonderland*. James Scott's *Frog Legs Rag* "combines the sentimental with the most glittering fireworks. It cannot be described. It must be heard. It touches all sides of American appreciation."[103]

Ragtime music, like folk music, is part of our shared American heritage. I think Miss Mason would have wanted it preserved as a national treasure, but that's only a guess.

During Miss Mason's time, Americans endured the San Francisco earthquake and fire, and New York City swelled with immigrants seeking a new life. Klezmer music found its way to America from Eastern Europe, as did other aspects of Yiddish culture.

To place Klezmer music in history, this would have been around the time that President McKinley was assassinated and Theodore Roosevelt took his place. Cotton candy, telephones, electric lights, and hot air balloon rides were invented. Miss Mason would have known of all or at least a few of these American events.

Our heritage is not entirely tangible—some of it is stored in our communal memory through patriotic songs, plays, and shared experience. As we look at folk songs, then, we Americans need to remember that our songs are a reflection of our history. It's wonderful to learn the English and French folk songs Miss Mason recommended, but I hope you won't leave out American folk songs altogether. We can sometimes be such sticklers for doing "what Charlotte Mason did" that we allow it to overshadow what is good and right for us personally. With Miss Mason's focus on personhood, I think we ought not to let that happen. Learning the music of our own past is as important as learning about the flowers and trees in our own city and neighborhood—because they all represent who we are and where we have come from. In this sense, we are being true to the spirit, not the letter, of a Charlotte Mason education. She lived in England, and most of us live in the United States. There will be slight variations in our musical choices, just as there would be if we were teaching in Germany instead of Turkey, or Russia instead of Canada.

Acoustic Ecologist Gordon Hempton says:

> I've been recording in Sri Lanka, for example. I spent a couple of weeks just recording the remote places there and the beautiful music that comes through the night, all the insects and frogs weaving deep textures. And then I listen to the folk music, and I hear the same thing all over again. Our music is just a reflection of who we are.[104]

Folk songs center us; they give us a sense of heritage and solidify our sense of place. That being the case, we will need to tackle the question: which folk songs should we study? AmblesideOnline has a wonderful list of choices for you, and if you go to the Library of Congress website and do a quick search, you may find even more. I've placed a list of folk songs in Appendix E, but here are a few American favorites arranged according to time period:

Settlement to 1763: "Bonny Barbara Allan"
The American Revolution (1763–1783): "Yankee Doodle"

The New Nation (1783–1815): "Hunters of Kentucky"
National Expansion (1815–1860): "Ho! For the Kansas Plains"
Civil War and Reconstruction (1861–1877): "John Brown's Body," "The Battle Hymn of the Republic"
Rise of Industrial America (1876–1900): "The Workers' Anvil"
Progressive Era to New Era (1900–1929): "You're a Grand Old Flag"
Great Depression/World War II (1929–1945): "Sunny California"

For an extensive list of American and multicultural folk songs with listening samples, check out songsforteaching.com/folk.

Every nation has its own folk songs. There are Polish folk songs like "Green Linden Tree," Russian folk songs like "Dark Eyes," Peruvian folk songs like "My Little Dove," and Japanese folk songs like the familiar "Sakura" (Cherry Blossom). Inuit folk songs were vocalized in the back of the throat to the accompaniment of box drums. Members of the Apache tribe used nasal singing accompanied by rattles and the Apache fiddle. You can dance the Kuratsa folk dance in the Philippines, the Cossack dance in Ukraine, and the Circassian Circle in France. Folk music often has hand motions or a "jig" of some sort attached to it, and including folk dancing can be a great way to break up the meatier part of your study schedule. Your students will be cheerful and exhilarated after folk song study and ready to buckle down for some more serious brain work that requires steady effort.

Today, American scholars no longer call the music from our cultural history "folk music." It is considered "American Roots Music." Just a tiny tweak in terminology, one might think, but I believe it's a more apt description of this particular form. Typically, folk music came to us from European musical roots, but as we all know, America is a melting pot of living ideas, cultures, and stories. If we expand the genre to include all roots music, we can learn the spirituals sung by African-American slaves in the Old South. We can include Native American music and Cajun music of Louisiana, with its lush French overtones, harmonica, and bluesy rhythms. This was music sung out in the cotton field or on the front porch while sipping cold lemonade in the hot summer sun. Expanding our study of folk music to include Native American rhythms (drum circles—always dedicated to God—and early Gospel music will add a richness to the study that you might miss if you only sing the nursery songs I listed above or a few choice sea shanties and patriotic songs.

Freedom is a thread that weaves its way through American folk music in such tunes as "We Shall Overcome" or "We Shall Not Be Moved." Woody Guthrie is our most famous folk music composer. Bessie Smith, Burl Ives, Muddy Waters, and Pete Seeger also stand out as leaders in American folk music history—especially Pete Seeger, whose gentle admonitions and kind spirit offer us a glimpse of America at its most compassionate and insightful.

The gentle, homey sounds of folk music found their way into Mark Twain's *Huckleberry Finn*, where he described a folk dance called "The Juba." Bruce Springsteen brought hints of Woody Guthrie into his album *The Ghost of Tom Joad*.[105]

Appalachian folk music is still around today, largely because Olive Dame Campbell popularized it in the early twentieth century. You can learn more about her story from the movie *The Songcatcher* and perhaps by visiting Brasstown, North Carolina, where her John C. Campbell Folk School is still in operation. They hold retreats and conferences at the Folk School where you can have experiences in non-competitive learning and community life that are joyful and enlivening. Located in scenic Brasstown, North Carolina, the Folk School offers year-round weeklong and weekend classes for adults in craft, art, music, dance, cooking, gardening, nature studies, photography and writing.[106]

Imagine spending a weekend learning reels, listening to fiddle and dulcimer music, and making pottery, leather crafts, weaving, and more. We Americans tend to forget that in days past working with the hands was vital to daily life. Bread must be made, vegetables grown, fruit picked, grain harvested. I hope one day to enjoy a weekend in Brasstown and listen for the echoes of Olive's folk song collection.

At folk societies across the country, you can hear live folk music performed, meet the performers, try out the instruments, and learn a bit about folk music. We used to attend folk music concerts here in our city, and our children were always drawn into the community. There was often a potluck dinner afterwards. Children were welcomed, and handicrafts were displayed. Our daughter played fiddle music and sometimes jammed with the musicians. Participating in folk music concerts forms even stronger connections with the community than merely attending would. Even if your children can only shake a tambourine or tap a triangle, audience participation is a must. In fact, I think these warm communities need our support if they are going to continue. We live in a society that moves too fast. We are the technology generation, and taking a step back to enjoy life as it once was can be crucial to developing a strong understanding of our historical roots.

The instruments most often used in traditional American folk music are tambourine, hammer dulcimer, fiddle, banjo, harmonica, spoons, guitar, accordion, flute, and drums.[107] Leading the pack, so to speak, is the country fiddle, which accompanies all dances, reels, and forms the backbone of the hearty traditional mountain music we all associate with folk songs. The more robust-sounding dulcimer, or hog fiddle, as some call it, was influenced by German, Norwegian, Swedish, and French instruments that were similar and brought to America by immigrants. Add in some Irish pipes, and you'll have that true folk instrumental sound.

If you really want to go all out in your studies and are somewhat crafty, you might have the children "make" a few of these instruments. I remember our children fastening two spoons together with rubber bands and trying to play them. A rectangular tissue box with rubber bands stretched over the hole in the middle and a paper towel roll attached to the top makes a great guitar for a preschooler. Pots and pans become drums, played jubilantly with a wooden spoon. Harmonicas are inexpensive, as are kazoos. You could have your own little folk music band and tour the neighborhood, singing *"Old Kentucky Home"* or *"Father Abraham."*

Folk dancing is rooted in the folk music of America, and of England as well. As immigration increased, America saw her German, Polish, and Czech immigrants transform the waltz and cotillion into the reel and square dances. At some point, the mandolin and banjo joined the party and mountain square dancing left the more formal British dances behind. The Sir Roger de Coverly dance became The Virginia Reel.[108] Couples switched partners more frequently to give young people a chance to get to know one another somewhere besides at church. The rest, as they say, is history.

Leon Litwick wrote a curriculum guide for students to study American Roots Music in depth. He took songs from all traditions—blues, folk, Gospel, country, Cajun, and Native American—and brought them together for students. His work is a great resource to help us as teachers to wrap our minds around the cultural significance of all of these musical genres. As we add "The

Thrill Is Gone," "If I Had a Hammer," "Oh Happy Day," "Walking the Floor Over You," and the drumming of traditional Native American music to our repertoire, our students will have a strong understanding of our American cultural heritage and as a result may enlarge their hearts toward people of other nationalities, cultures, and beliefs. This is one way to conquer potential xenophobia within our communities, too.

Folk music historian Alan Lomax once said:

> The best song-makers for children are the folk, whose rhymes are rubbed clean and hard against the bone of life, whose fantasies are heart-warming and fertile because they rise out of billions of accumulated hours of living with and caring for children . . . the jingles, riddles, silly ballads, wistful lullabies, jiggy tunes and game songs belonging to the children of the American frontier will one day make a book far more warm and witty than the traditional Mother Goose.[109]

While we owe a great debt to Alan Lomax for preserving folk music for us, he has been accused of stealing copyrights from the original composers, and it's a fair accusation. He snatched them up shortly before he wrote his books. Regarding this situation, Woody Guthrie said the following:

> This song is copyrighted in the U.S. under seal of copyright #154085, for a period of 28 years, and anybody caught singin' it without our permission will be mighty good friends of ourn, cause we don't give a dern. Publish it. Write it. Sing it. Swing to it. Yodel it. We wrote it, that's all we wanted to do.

This is the heartbeat behind folk music—it's the music of the people, the music that arose out of dusty streets as sweat was wiped across furrowed brows. Lynn Bruce of AmblesideOnline says folk songs help us get to the good parts of our shared humanness, that they are the doorway through which children find their own voices, and I agree. Members of the National Children's Folksong Repository have said that folk music "lives in memory alone, and like the proverbial river into which one can never step twice, it is always in the process of becoming." Like fairy tales passed down through oral tradition, folk songs have been passed down through a shared history from mother to daughter, father to son, village to village. And the shared experience is slightly different with each telling.

Marley Spencer, a young girl raised on Charlotte Mason's educational methods, had this to say:

> If classical music is of the head, and religious music is of the heart, folk music is of the hands—cracked and dirty hands. Hands that work, hands that love, and hands that are never too tired to pick up a guitar or a fiddle and tell a great story. If classical and religious music helps us focus on a higher plane, folk music keeps us firmly rooted in this one— the one where we walk and eat and play with our fellow creatures.[110]

Whether they are classic jump rope chants, clapping songs like "Miss Mary Mac" and "Say, Say, My Playmate," or simple folk songs, the folk music of the past always provokes laughter and togetherness. You may want to create a peaceful atmosphere for your folk song study by lighting a fire in an outdoor firepit and gathering friends and neighbors for an evening of singing and storytelling. It may feel awkward at first, but these gatherings could become a favorite autumn tradition and are a great way to preserve our national heritage for future generations.

KLEZMER MUSIC

My family first heard klezmer music at a free concert featuring a local symphony member, a clarinet player. The clarinet is the backbone of the klezmer sound, and once you listen to klezmer, it just feels right to have that silky clarinet crooning throughout. The word *klezmer* literally translates as "vessel of music." It began as an offshoot of Jewish religious music in the Eastern European region where Ashkenazi Jews settled. This was party music—perfect for dancing, toe-tapping, and cheering up. It's haunting and lively and fun but with a twinge of sadness. To me, klezmer music is the wailing of survival, the cathartic howl of a wronged people. It has grown in popularity in recent years, and I'm happy about that as a person of Jewish descent. Klezmer is the folk music of the gypsies and displaced Jewish people of Eastern Europe. My people.

Klezmer music thrived during the period of immigration from Eastern Europe to America, roughly 1880–1924. Once here, these new citizens quickly assimilated into American culture, striving to retain their Jewish heritage through Yiddish language, drama, poetry, story, and song. Here is where things got interesting. Klezmer music incorporated a new type of music—American jazz—into its fast-paced dance music, and a brand new genre appeared, perfect for wedding receptions and parties.

At one time, klezmer music was called "Freilech music" or "happy music," but there are undertones of sadness and melancholy in true klezmer music, too. It is said to mimic the human voice and experience. All sorts of dances, from mazurkas to polkas to the Jewish hora and even the tango were originally accompanied by klezmer-style music.

Typically, klezmer music was performed on clarinet, violin, accordion, and bass. Its original composers and performers came from Romania, Bulgaria, and Russia. If you want a change of pace from typical American or English folk songs or even French folk songs (Miss Mason encouraged learning French songs, too), try taking a week or two to learn about klezmer music. You might even incorporate learning a folk dance or two—maybe the hora or the polka. It will enliven your folk song study tremendously to get the children dancing and singing together.

JAZZ

While it isn't exactly "folk music," jazz was determined by the United States government to be "a rare and valuable national American treasure to which we should devote our attention, support, and resources to make certain it is preserved, understood, and promulgated." (This comes from a bill proposed by Representative John Conyers, Jr., in 1987.) Well, that makes it official. Jazz is part of our American heritage and it should also rest in this valued space in our shared cultural history.

Jazz is difficult to pin down. It's loaded with syncopation and relies heavily on improvisation. Essentially, each individual performer decides what jazz is as he or she plays. There are certain key elements: blues piano, soulful melodies, driving trumpets (a throwback to marching bands), soft and syncopated drum beats, often using brushes, with an underlying driving beat. You may hear melodies and countermelodies at the same time. You may notice that chords are more subtle and regular rhythms are gone. Some jazz music has its roots in Scott Joplin's ragtime songs, while other pieces grew out of the call and response songs of early slave laborers on Southern plantations.

I believe it is important to remember the contributions immigrants have made to American culture, and jazz music cuts through to the marrow of the tragic indignity and horrors of slavery that permeated our early American society. The sinister thread of racism that is still tearing at the fiber of society today has its roots in the enslavement of Africans. We cannot obliterate racism singlehandedly, but music has a strange capacity to create unity and promote peace. I hope we will one day free our land completely from racism and celebrate one another's gifts and talents and the cultural influences we each bring to our culture.

Rather than ignore slavery or hope that eventually we can forget about the horrifying mistakes we made as a nation, I believe celebrating jazz music as a part of our educational journey is one way we can bring restoration and healing to society. While we celebrate the contributions of Dizzy Gillespie, Louis Armstrong, Duke Ellington, and countless others to our American music heritage, we are, in a small way, tearing down the strongholds that have emboldened racism in America.

Music is the art which is most nigh to tears and memory.

—*Oscar Wilde*

Chapter Fourteen

On Clouds of Great Glory:
Hymn and Choral Study

It is time for hymn singing, and indeed for any good music. It seems to me that all music, except dance, opera, and comic music, is a boon on Sundays, and elevates the children's minds.

—Mrs. Stanton, *"The Child Depicted by Poets," Parents' Review*

A hush fell over the congregation as the lights dimmed throughout the cavernous cathedral. The choir stood just outside the double doors that led to the center aisle—candles lit, robes and cassocks on, shiny black patent leather shoes tapping gently across the marble floor, hushed whispers of last-minute instructions. It was time! The choir assistants opened the double doors, and Meg Woodruff and I (being the shortest choir members) led the procession down the aisle, solemnly singing Benjamin Britten's "Hodie Christus natus est," a cappella. My palms were clammy, and my arms were sore from holding the candle straight out in front of me. We had to walk the length of the church, then around the altar, behind it, and back again before processing up the stairs to the choir loft to officially begin the midnight service on Christmas Eve. It was a holy moment. I never forgot it.

I could never overestimate the power and the value of a choral education. You cannot manufacture choral learning from a book at home. If at all possible, I urge you to have your students form or join a choir and learn some of the masterful choral arrangements of the past. I fell into choir almost by accident after my parents put me into a private parochial school, St. Michael School in Dallas, Texas, back in the 1970s. I had been somewhat traumatized by a teacher in a public school. It turned out to be an isolated incident—it was actually a wonderful little neighborhood school—but as one thing leads to another on this journey we call life, I ended up at a school across town, dressed in a red, white, and blue sailor suit, with only thirty students in each grade. Most of my new friends were in the church choir. I was not even a member of a church—any church. But I asked to join my friends, and my parents said yes. Thus began a beautiful journey, led by Paul Lindsey Thomas, choir director extraordinaire for St. Michael and All Angels Episcopal Church.

We wore blue beanies that first year and long blue robes with white ruffled collars. The robes made a gigantic impression on me, an unchurched third grader. And it was a tremendous bonding experience. By fourth grade, we had graduated to maroon robes with white cassocks. We each had our favorite anthems. Mine was "O, Lord Most Merciful." Every week, we led the singing at the smaller service in the "little chapel," as they called it. I memorized the Beatitudes by staring at them each week, as they were imprinted on the stained glass windows of that chapel.

I learned to harmonize, to read music, to follow directions, to follow a conductor. These are pleasant memories even today. I could still name the girls in that choir. Some of them I still consider friends today. Each year, we got a new medal to wear around our necks on a colored ribbon. It was exciting to "graduate" to the next level at the end of the year. We worked hard. We wanted to impress Mr. Thomas, and we wanted to sing beautifully for God. There was an awe-inspiring childhood innocence in the air. As Mrs. Stanton said in her *Parents' Review* article "The Child Depicted by Poets":

> All experience points to the possession in childhood of a fresh spiritual life, which becomes more or less soiled in the common life of the world. . . . The man blushes to remember his boyish illusions, not because they were foolish, but because he is no longer pure-hearted enough to have them.[111]

As I said earlier, when my children were old enough, we placed them in a similar choir in North Carolina. The Choir School at St. Peters was strict, the instruction rigorous. The choir director, Ben Outen, had high expectations, and our children were stretched musically and mentally. The Choir School held classes where students learned music theory. They, too, progressed through levels, but they were not merely awarded for staying in choir another year. You had to earn these ribbons by learning your theory and passing a test. The Choir School went on tour every spring—to churches in New England or Florida or Virginia. Every few years, they traveled to the UK, and one of our daughters was in choir that year, too. It was a privilege to participate in the Choir School, as well as a challenge.

In his book *Choral Technique and Interpretation*, Henry Coward outlined the qualities of a great choral director:

> the conductor must have power to inspire, incite, and command—a kind of personal magnetism, which makes his persuasive will law. To get this power two things are necessary. First, he must be so thoroughly master of the work in hand that the choir have confidence in him and will follow him in everything. Second, he must be an enthusiast in his work. To be the master he must be at the service of all. His zeal must infect his followers.[112]

There is that pesky word again—enthusiasm. In order to interest students in their work (*piacere*) and in order to enable them to take delight in it (*movere*), the teacher's enthusiasm, confidence, and zeal are of the utmost importance.

The practice of hymn study in a Charlotte Mason school or homeschool is outlined in several different *Parents' Review* articles as well as Miss Mason's volumes. This is exciting work. It's putting children in touch with the King of Kings and Lord of Lords. It's offering them a way to reach the heart of God through worship. This is, perhaps, one of the most important facets of music education and even of the entire Charlotte Mason method. If you take a big picture view of her volumes, you can see that her heart was beating madly for the children to form relationships with God, the Creator of all things known and unknown, above ground, beneath the soil, in the sky, and beyond the clouds. Here are a few key quotes on the matter, taken from the *Parents' Review* article "The Religious Training of Children at Home" (no author listed):

No child of mine, unless of its own free will, should learn a whole hymn on Sunday. It is a very common and delightful custom to repeat hymns on Sunday—every one of the family saying something—and you will say, 'Hymns ought to be learnt.' Yes indeed, they ought; but must it be a whole hymn? Would not two verses carefully said be as acceptable, and the rest of the hymn could be read, and more of it learnt another Sunday.

The children may get up later [on Sunday], having no lessons before breakfast; but I invariably hear one or other of them playing and singing hymns soon after eight.

When my children outgrew their baby prayers, I gave them a little book with a list of subjects for prayer and left them to find their own words. It is such a list as any parent might draw up for their children. I also asked them to learn suitable verses of Psalms and hymns for prayer and praise—single verses which they could use at any time. And in the little book there are plenty of blank pages where they can write these down.[113]

Miss Mason wanted children to spend time glorifying God through singing. That much is clear. But which hymns did she have her students sing? To get at that is a bit difficult. There are currently 52 Anglican hymnals in existence, and they cover about 140 years' worth of hymns. That's 7,000 different texts with more than 18,000 text and music combinations. Where do we begin? There is a website, oremus.org, that lists all 52 hymnals, and its owners are endeavoring to collect for us all the hymns represented among them. Because I believe Miss Mason was fond of following the church calendar year as most Anglicans did, I think she may have used *The Church Hymnal for the Christian Year* (1917) as her source. With my own children, I used the Anglican hymnal from 1940 because I grew up singing its hymns, and you may want to use your own personal favorite, too. That is completely up to you. (I know most who follow Charlotte Mason's methods today are not Anglican.) But since we are trying to bring forth as authentic a Charlotte Mason education as possible here, I believe we can narrow the search down to two: *The Church Hymnal for* the *Christian Year* and *A Church of England Hymn Book*, which was produced by Reverend Godfrey Thring, who is mentioned in Miss Mason's volumes and in several *Parents' Review* articles as a trusted colleague. These versions are both available at oremus.org.

Now for the nitty gritty—how do we study hymns anyway? It's much easier if you attend a church where hymns are sung weekly, but if you do not, there are plenty of YouTube videos and MIDI files available online to help you, the teacher, learn these hymns. Buy a hymnal. Listen to the tunes online or at church. Begin singing. Repeat. That's all there is to it. Well, perhaps not all. If you play the piano, you can accompany your children as they sing. You can also teach them sight-singing through solfège. That way, once they are strong enough at note-reading, they can sing in parts. What a glorious sound! Children singing in four-part harmony (or two if you don't have any older boys whose voices have changed). What a pleasing aroma toward God the worship of children must be.

Our Hymn Study Journey

We began hymn study when our oldest was around seven years old, with little musical training beyond the worship choruses we learned at our modern church. We started with a simple hymn: "Now the Day is Over."

Now the day is over,
Night is drawing nigh,
Shadows of the evening
Steal across the sky.

That's it. Just four lines. There are many verses, all available at cyberhymnal. org, so I picked a couple more for them to memorize. After they got the general tune down securely, I tried adding in an alto line to see if they were able to harmonize. They were! We sang this hymn every night together as a family before bedtime. It quickly became a lovely, loving nighttime routine. Here are a few more verses:

Now the darkness gathers,
Stars begin to peep,
Birds, and beasts and flowers
Soon will be asleep.

Jesus, give the weary
Calm and sweet repose;
With Thy tenderest blessing
May mine eyelids close.

Comfort those who suffer,
Watching late in pain;
Those who plan some evil
From their sin restrain.

Through the long night watches
May Thine angels spread
Their white wings above me,
Watching round my bed.

When the morning wakens,
Then may I arise
Pure, and fresh, and sinless
In Thy holy eyes.

After we learned "Now the Day is Over," we tackled a couple of more difficult hymns: "Onward, Christian Soldiers" and "Come, Labor On." These were motivational for our family as we went about our day. At times, the children balked at their studies. Some of it was grunt work: memorizing times tables, learning to write in cursive. These were difficult tasks requiring steady effort. It was good to have two hymns that reminded us we are called to steady effort, hard work, and to stand until the end.

A few other favorites are "A Mighty Fortress is Our God," "Ye Watchers and Ye Holy Ones," "Let All Mortal Flesh Keep Silence," "Praise to the Lord," "Now Thank We All Our God," "We Gather Together" (a Thanksgiving hymn), and "Crown Him with Many Crowns." But your needs will be different, just as every family is unique and each child a person with different needs than his brother or sister. Ask the Lord what hymns He has for your family, or you can follow the AmblesideOnline schedule for hymn study.

Singing hymns will bring a delightful peace to the atmosphere in your home or school. It can be a balm to your souls to join your voices in song. Singing requires breath, and just as God placed the breath inside Adam and Eve, we take in His glory and goodness by the power of the Holy Spirit. What we give back upon our own outgoing breath is our worship. May you breathe songs of praise to our God and bless Him with your voice. I will leave you with a psalm.

PSALM 150

Praise ye the Lord.

Praise God in his sanctuary:
> praise him in the firmament of his power.
Praise him for his mighty acts:
> praise him according to his excellent greatness.
Praise him with the sound of the trumpet:
> praise him with the psaltery and harp.
Praise him with the timbrel and dance:
> praise him with stringed instruments and organs.
Praise him upon the loud cymbals:
> praise him upon the high sounding cymbals.

Let every thing that hath breath praise the Lord. Praise ye the Lord.

Praise ye the Lord.

Bach opens a vista to the universe. After experiencing him, people feel there is meaning to life after all.

—Helmut Walcha

Developing Open Hearts and Eager Expectation: Lingering Long and Leaving Well Fed

Mournful and yet grand is the destiny of the artist.

—*Franz Liszt*

Charlotte Mason believed children benefitted far more from hearing music performed live than listening to it on a gramophone or any other recording device of the day (iPod, MP3 player, Spotify, SoundCloud, iTunes). A certain amount of awe arises from attending a symphony performance—the hush that falls over the audience after the musicians have finished tuning up and fall silent, the effort it takes to dress up a bit and drive to the venue, the way a child's ears are attuned to the acoustics and eyes transfixed upon the stage. The atmosphere is heightened with anticipation, the sound more full and rich as its waves bounce across a large auditorium with a high ceiling. Here is what Miss Mason said about it:

> Boys and girls living in London have great opportunities. Concerts are often arranged especially for them, and sometimes professional musicians are engaged to perform the works at some private house where there is a branch of the Parents' Union School. Children can be taken to the Sunday Concerts at the Queen's Hall or Albert Hall. It is not necessary for them to stay all through the performance—take them

out after the finest composition has been played. But, as I said before about pictures, it is not much use taking them to concerts unless they have some previous idea of what they are going to hear. Familiarity with the work means enjoyment of the finished performance.[114]

Gordon Hempton believes quiet places are secure places that calm us. I agree. When the world is hushed and I am alone with only the humming of the dishwasher in my ears at the end of a long day, I can feel the tension drain out of me. I come alive to the world around me when everything grows quiet. Hempton says:

> This happens in nature when a deer, for example, has to drink out of a creek and then the noise of the creek blocks its ability to make surveillance, so it tries to compensate quickly with glances with its eyes, and then it drinks and then it moves back into a quiet place so it can continue to be secure. Isn't it amazing that our concert halls, our churches, places like that, they're quiet places? They're places where we can feel secure, secure enough that we can open up and be receptive and truly listen. And when we're truly listening, we also have to anticipate that we might become changed by what we have heard.[115]

I could recount to you the dozens of concerts we attended during our children's formative years, but there are a few that stand out. We took them to hear an early music consort perform at Davidson College. They were fascinated by the instruments—a hurdy-gurdy, a viola da gamba, and some early woodwind instruments whose names now escape me. After the performance, the musicians were available for questions, and most of the children present wanted nothing more than to touch the instruments, to see them up close. Of course they did. This is how children learn!

Another time, we received the Virginia Symphony packet with eagerness and listened to the cassette tape religiously in anticipation of the concert a few weeks later. The children absorbed these pieces until they became a part of the fabric of their souls. They were hooked, and we had not even attended the concert yet. I decided to make it an important event, so we dressed up, spruced up our hair, and the girls even got a little smear of lip gloss for the occasion. We got to the performance hall, and they soaked in every note. Unfortunately, as I mentioned earlier, the students around them who were herded onto buses for the event did not receive the same careful preparation and were bouncy and loud throughout the concert. The feast was set before them, but they were not taught to enjoy such delicacies, I'm afraid!

The story doesn't end there, however. We continued to listen to the cassette recording and vowed that we would attend the Friday morning concert since it had been difficult to hear the music over the din of excitable students earlier in the week. But when Friday came, I completely forgot we were going to head back. The performance started at 11:00 a.m., and I realized my mistake at about 10:40. But the trip would take at least twenty minutes! I said, "Oh no! I forgot we were going to go back to the symphony again! Hurry! Grab your shoes! Hop in the car!" They did. I popped in the cassette tape, hurled the van down the driveway, and on we went. We all still vividly remember flying down the highway to the tune of "the Lone Ranger song" (the *William Tell Overture*), which was on the program that morning. Rossini's *Overture* has become our theme song for whenever we are running late because—you guessed it—we got there just in time for the lights to dim and the concert to begin. Our grand adventure was a success!

While attending live performances is important, there's something more to be treasured by learning an instrument and performing with an ensemble or orchestra for yourself. Our children learned various instruments—cello, clarinet, recorder, viola, piano, violin—but our eldest daughter is the only one who performed on an orchestral instrument (violin). She was in youth orchestras, fiddle groups, did recording gigs, and wrote the opening music for a TV series. She was quite a busy student! Now she sings opera and scores video games. Her early experiences were formative and gave her not only the inclination to pursue music as a career but a priceless gift—the joy and love of music. Our other children also performed in operas and learned to play piano and guitar. Our youngest is an amazing drummer. Our eldest son writes beautiful music and has just completed his degree at The Boston Conservatory. The steps you take right now, today, will swing open the door to a future full of music appreciation, of joy and beauty, and you never know—possibly a career in the arts. Precept upon precept, step by step, implement the recommendations Miss Mason and those she entrusted with the music education of her students made and you will see the fruit of your labors in immeasurable ways as they grow and mature.

I recently listened to a podcast from the kind folks at the Circe Institute, hosted by David Kern. John Hodges, Director of the Center for Western Studies, was sharing on the topic of music appreciation, and he had some profound thoughts on the matter that I believe are important. In his opinion, we humans can only decide what music we enjoy using our own life experiences. If we are the ones perched on the throne of our lives, if we are the deciders, the ones who get to tell others which music is good and which is not as good, we will constantly err because we can only base our decisions on our own personal affections, which have been, in turn, based on our own personal life experiences—the good, the bad, and the ugly.

Each one of us individually will choose something different, and that something will generally degrade over time to become the lowest common denominator, as it has in the field of pop music. What was cringe-worthy and lacking in musical quality back in the 1950s has degraded and become much worse, as Miley Cyrus twerks her way across the stage, barely clothed, and violence is glorified by the hip hop "artists" of our time. Will we wake up and notice this degradation? It seems each successive generation chooses to push the envelope just a little bit further, and instead of returning to artistic depth and complexity, we are sinking deeper into the mire. But is there an antidote?

John Hodges believes we need to see ourselves as stewards representing someone higher than ourselves and learn to "minister to things" to make them more as God intended before the fall of man. Instead of remaking the world into our image, becoming increasingly blind to the natural relationships God created for us, we can remember the beauty of harmony and consider that music may well have been created as a metaphor for something much larger than ourselves—the harmony of God, the Trinity, expressions of truth, of nature, of glory. But this can only happen if we take ourselves off the throne and become stewards instead of masters. What a simple thing, a decision to yield to God's will in our lives, yet we struggle so much to do it.

In all likelihood, God did not create music to appease our worldly appetites, as is the case when we see ourselves as masters of the world rather than stewards. If music was created for the purpose of describing the cosmic dance, of seeing the harmonies of our souls rightly, there is a weighty responsibility here. Hodges says we must see music from a sacramental view, as a direct connection between the physical world and the spiritual world. Music can transcend the ordinary and lift us to extraordinary heights on the whisper of mere sound waves.

Art and sculpture are centered in one place, but music soars on the air—literally. This means the composer, artist, and musician have a great responsibility toward God. But not every composer even knew or had a relationship with God. This is where grace enters the picture. He will anoint whom He will anoint. God's grace is available to every human being, and you never quite know what to expect with our great and glorious God. He surprises us by sending the Holy Spirit to unexpected places. And His gifts and callings are given regardless of repentance, meaning He pours out gifts upon us and does not recall them simply because we err or use them unwisely. We see some treat their musical gifts recklessly and others with tender care. Thus is life on this wild earth. But we, as listeners, would do well to make informed decisions about what we choose to put before our ears as well as our eyes.

Hodges gives us hope that our children can and will reach for higher living and deeper learning and attain it. He says that to capture the imagination of a reluctant learner you have to begin with short pieces and come at them with a sense of mystery, of longing to know and understand the motivations of the man or woman who composed the piece. This requires a bit of preparation on our parts, but only a bit—a quiet "listen for the tide rising in this section" or "here it sounds like the stomping of feet or the soaring of doves, doesn't it?" Most listeners won't want to work hard, not at first. But our impoverished taste needs time to grow accustomed to the meatier, more complex music of ages past. As I've said before, you may be raising a future composer, conductor, opera singer, or symphony musician. We owe each child access to a veritable feast. While it may require some hard effort on our parts to present them with every aspect of a Charlotte Mason music education, from earliest habits of attention to nature sounds to later sight-singing, solfège, instrument lessons, and attention to form, instrumentation, and composers, I believe the child's growing appreciation for and participation in a life filled with music is worth the hard work it will require to present it to them.

We present music to a child in much the same way we present all living ideas—it must rise on the air around them, stand securely as a foundation beneath them. Miss Mason says:

> Ideas may invest, as an atmosphere, rather than strike as a weapon.
> 'The idea may exist in a clear, distinct, definite form, as that of a circle
> in the mind of a geometrician; or it may be a mere instinct, a vague
> appetency towards something, . . . like the impulse which fills the young
> poet's eyes with tears, he knows not why.' To excite this 'appetency
> towards something'—towards things lovely, honest, and of good report,
> is the earliest and most important ministry of the educator. How shall
> these indefinite ideas which manifest themselves in appetency be
> imparted? They are not to be given of set purpose, nor taken at set
> times. They are held in that thought-environment which surrounds the
> child as an atmosphere, which he breathes as his breath of life; and this
> atmosphere in which the child inspires his unconscious ideas of right
> living emanates from his parents.[116]

Miss Mason embraces the visions of Plato and Coleridge when it comes
to the importance of vitalizing ideas. Plato says, "An idea is a distinguishable
power, self-affirmed, and seen in its unity with the Eternal Essence." And
Hodges agrees. In his Circe podcast, he says music is transcendent, leading the
listener to become more high-minded, more attuned to the idea that there is
something larger than us, an adventure more grand than the low-minded life
we so often settle for. We can connect with the Eternal, if we will but make
some small effort in that direction.

Coleridge says, "Events and images, the lively and spirit-stirring machinery
of the external world, are like light, and air, and moisture to the seed of the
mind, which would else rot and perish." Studying music nourishes the mind,
the senses. It requires discipline, analysis, patience, and hard effort, but it
rewards with joy, passion, a sense of accomplishment, and beauty. We ought
to enter its study with humility, as we would enter Heaven for the first time—
bearing in mind that we are in the presence of great genius and of the powerful
unction of the Holy Spirit.

Puccini once said "Inspiration is an awakening, a quickening of all man's
faculties, and it is manifested in all high artistic achievements." Only God can
inspire a man to greatness. Without Him, we can do nothing, as the Bible tells

us. But more than that, *with* Him, we can produce high-minded works of great artistic achievement. Acknowledging God in all we do can infuse our art with purpose and beauty and glory. But lest we get puffed up with pride as if we are the sole bearers of His glorious light, remember the words of Charlotte Mason:

> the great recognition, that God the Holy Spirit is Himself, personally, the Imparter of knowledge, the Instructor of youth, the Inspirer of genius, is a conception so far lost to us that we should think it distinctly irreverent to conceive of the divine teaching as co-operating with ours in a child's arithmetic lesson, for example. But the Florentine mind of the Middle Ages went further than this: it believed, not only that the seven Liberal Arts were fully under the direct outpouring of the Holy Ghost, but that every fruitful idea, every original conception, whether in Euclid, or grammar, or music, was a direct inspiration from the Holy Spirit, without any thought at all as to whether the person so inspired named himself by the name of God or recognized whence his inspiration came.[117]

"Every fruitful idea, every original conception..." God is the divine inspirer of all beauty, whether in music, math, science, or literature. He is the One Whose gifts are poured out among us, no matter who we are or what we believe or even if we don't believe. It's a concept as fascinating as infinity.

Music is our response or reaction to life, nature, the universe, to God. I could speak for an hour on the wonders of a tiny cell or the mighty power of a waterfall. We could talk about science—the incredible intricacy of the organ systems of the human body and the elemental composition of the earth. These are all glorious, intricate, delicate designs from a loving Creator. And then there is art. A sculpture, painting, or piece of music does not create itself. The components are all there, surely, but the magnificence of each piece comes from the hand of a creator—a co-conspirator with God who takes inspiration, as Brahms says, and mixes it with craftsmanship to form something beautiful, something of high value. This is an incredible realization. Every invention, every work of art, every piece of music, required both God's inspiration and man's cooperation. We are allowed to participate in the divine dance that is creation. It's enough to make me want to stop writing immediately and try to compose a song or paint a painting, just to see and acknowledge God's anointing upon *me*. But that's the beauty of His design. He crafted me for writing and Bach for composing and Alexander Graham Bell for inventing and Jonas Salk for medical cures. We need only get in touch with the Master's plan, to sit at His feet and receive what He has for each one of us, and then imagine the glory that will come of that inspiration–craftsmanship combination.

This is one reason I believe apprenticeships and mentoring are important in education. We need master craftsmen to take junior craftsmen on to help them hone their craft the way medieval artists did. If you believe your child or one of your students has the capacity to become a great composer or performer or musician, I hope you will encourage him or her to find a mentor who will encourage your child's growth and maturity in the craft.

Charlotte Mason's Great Recognition did not end with her admonition that God is over every subject, and indeed, over all creation. She connected the relationship to education:

> But once the intimate relation, the relation of Teacher and taught in
> all things of the mind and spirit, be fully recognized, our feet are set
> in a large room; there is space for free development in all directions,
> and this free and joyous development, whether of intellect or heart, is
> recognized as a Godward movement.[118]

This really is the point of our Charlotte Mason education—to set our children's feet in a large room and allow space for free development in all directions. We might not know which direction they will turn for vocational purposes as adults, but that need not matter in the least. We are putting before them a great feast of living ideas and their only task is to leave well fed. When it comes to music education, that means we have offered them strong relationships with every major composer, including the composer's story, music, country of origin, acquaintances and the events that happened during his or her lifetime. It includes learning musical form and instrumentation, solfège, folk songs and their cultural roots, hymns and choral study, opera, jazz, and the science of sound. It includes mastering the art of music composition to the extent possible for each student, and it includes learning to play an instrument, the basics of conducting, sight-reading, and piano.

We are called to "come before Him with thanksgiving and extol Him with music and song." When the disciples were all in one accord, "speaking to one another in psalms, hymns, and spiritual songs, singing and making music," His power was poured out among them. And on that final day described in Revelation, we will sing a new song, proclaiming, "Worthy is the Lamb that was slain." Music has been with us since the dawn of time in this wild universe, and so it will be with us at the end of our days. A Charlotte Mason music education includes all the components I mentioned above and just one more—the acknowledgment that all good gifts come from the Father of Lights Who does not alter or change and in Whom is no shadow of turning. May we graciously and humbly lay out a feast for our students that breathes life and joy and beauty into their willing and eager hearts.

Let this be the mother's key to the whole of the education of each boy and each girl; not of her children; the Divine Spirit does not work with nouns of multitude, but with each single child. Because He is infinite, the whole world is not too great a school for this indefatigable Teacher, and because He is infinite, He is able to give the whole of his infinite attention for the whole time to each one of his multitudinous pupils. We do not sufficiently rejoice in the wealth that the infinite nature of our God brings to each of us.

—Charlotte Mason, Parents and Children

Epilogue

Practical Application

The instrument, whether it be a piano or a violin or a voice, is only a medium for that strange and impalpable something which to the majority of mankind seems as necessary as the breath of Heaven.

—*Mrs. Spencer Curwen*

Much of what we have discussed has been theoretical and even philosophical at times. It is important to understand why this method was designed, why Miss Mason crafted her ideas so carefully that it took six volumes to fully flesh them out for future generations. We need to know the "what" as well—we should immerse ourselves in the study of these composers' lives so that they become such a part of the fiber of our beings that their work is absorbed effortlessly by our children or students. But there is a nitty-gritty to the "how."

In teaching my children, I tried to remember these three things and even meditate on them so that I never forgot them. Our main goal is to give our children:

1) something to love
2) something to do, and
3) something to think about.

We ought to keep this in mind for every subject we teach. It's the anchor.

If we are proffering these three things to our children, we will in the end find they have been well fed and all the more so if we have planned the journey in such a way as to allow for them to reach for the knowledge themselves rather than having it handed to them in tidy morsels, ready for consumption.

SOMETHING TO LOVE

I think we've covered this category at great length already, but let me just reiterate that a child will fall in love with music as easily and mysteriously as an infant draws its first breath. We need only to place the masterpieces within the child's reach with a solid background on the composer to provide this.

SOMETHING TO DO

Learning to play an instrument, read music, compose, replace strings or reeds, practice, listen, create—these are integral pieces to the music appreciation puzzle. The student needs to take action, to be an active listener, an attentive rememberer, and a careful performer. Passively listening without any effort will not yield much in the way of true knowledge and the attainment of joy and life.

SOMETHING TO THINK ABOUT

Here we reach for the heart of a true learning experience with Charlotte Mason. She wanted to produce great thinkers who imbibe true knowledge. Students need time to ruminate on all the ideas they are taking in, so we need to make sure we offer the space for introspection and connection, to give our students time to wrestle with ideas, time to create, time to merely sit and think about the music and how it is affecting them.

Here are a few more practical things to keep in mind as you embark on your music appreciation journey with your students.

1) If you live in a city large enough to have a symphony, attend concerts with

your children. Often.

2) If you are able to attend live concerts, contact the symphony office and ask them for a study guide, some web links, recordings, samples, and maybe even a tour of the concert hall or venue. Find out what to wear, and lay out special clothes for each child the night before the performance. Make it a special event for them.

3) Go to park concerts whenever possible. Fresh air, fresh fruit, something bubbly, a blanket, some pillows, sunsets, and lilting classical music will help you make a memory.

4) If you live near a university that has a music program, go to as many recitals as you can. They are usually free, and you and your children will learn what individual instruments sound like. You can learn together. And don't forget to congratulate the student afterwards. Recitals are difficult!

5) Listen to your local classical radio station in the car and at home, or if you have Spotify or iTunes or something else, load in one composer at a time and delve deeply into his or her music, life, times, place, etc.

6) Have Composer Study parties. We used to celebrate certain composers' birthdays by hosting parties where we did a scavenger hunt or a treasure hunt, using clues from the composer's life to lead to the next piece of the puzzle. It's not an educational task, but it's fun. There's always cake, laughter, and effortless learning when you least expect it. And the children never forget what they've learned because it was a special event where they were in charge of seeking out the information rather than the teacher droning on and on and the student regurgitating the facts on a test at the end of the term. My favorite party was held on the night our local opera company was giving away free tickets to *La Bohème* to anyone who dressed in 1800s costumes. We got all the kids dressed up and got the best seats in the house. It was spectacular.

7) Find the best recordings of the very best composers of all time. There are many ways to accomplish this. Check out the websites in the appendix for a

great head start. Then, listen, listen, listen. Spend some focused time listening to the same piece each day, listening for tone, style, dynamics, musicality, and, of course, for fun. It may help to keep a placard with the current composer's name written on it beside your school table or desk as you listen so your students don't forget who they're listening to.

8) Talk about music. Talk about how to read music, what sharps and flats are, what the different rests look like. Draw them. Draw notes. Practice clapping rhythms. Create a staff and write your own music. Learn how to play an instrument and practice some simple tunes by your favorite composer. Have a favorite composer. Know who your favorite composer is because you have listened to many and decided for yourself. (If you don't know where to begin, try Mozart, Beethoven, Bach, Brahms, Mendelssohn, Johann Strauss, Jr., Rossini, or Tchaikovsky. For opera, Puccini and Verdi. For piano music, Chopin or Liszt. For modern music, Debussy or Stravinsky. I'm leaving out a lot of really special music in between, but this is a great start.)

MRS. CURWEN'S GUIDE TO AGE-APPROPRIATE MUSIC LESSONS

Miss Mason mentions a helpful resource for music education, Annie Jessy Curwen's piano method *The Child Pianist: Being a Practical Course of the Elements of Music*. The full Teacher's Guide to this curriculum is available online for download at archive.org and is well worth reading. Here are Curwen's recommendations for early music lessons. (I quoted some of this in chapter two.)

STAGE 1: BIRTH TO NURSERY

Surrounding your children with music from birth to age four or five by singing to them while rocking them is the first step in a child's music education. It allows the very young child to associate music with the comfort, pleasure, and the sweetness of resting in safety in Mom or Dad's lap.

The musical nurse, who croons old ditties while rocking the children to sleep, or dandles them on her knee to the well-marked rhythm of a country dance, is a powerful factor in their musical development, and such music lessons should be made a part of nursery training long before schoolroom or governess is dreamt of.[119]

STAGE 2: KINDERGARTEN

During this stage, rote-singing by ear and action songs are recommended so that children can get rhythm and melody stored in their minds and find pleasure in learning several songs that will remain with them always. This stage is filled with fun, concrete learning, movements and hand motions, and lots of laughter. Two books for this stage—Crane's Baby's Opera and Baby's Bouquet—were chosen for the programmes. These two books are available online. (See appendix for details.)

While children are singing by ear, marching to well-accented tunes, or performing the rhythmical movements of action songs, they are learning music in the concrete, and laying up in their minds a store of experiences to which the pianoforte teacher can appeal when the more formal systematic study of music commences.[120]

STAGE 3: TONIC SOL-FA

Singing class is next in Curwen's schedule. And the best introduction to reading music in her opinion included tonic sol-fa:

The introduction to notation, or "reading music," should be made in the singing class, where the children, unhindered by the manipulation of an instrument, can give their whole attention to the symbols which stand for the facts with which they made practical acquaintance while singing by ear. Here the question arises, "What symbols shall we use?" The easiest, surely; the letter-notation of the Tonic Sol-fa Method.[121]

STAGE 4: PIANO LESSONS

The child of eight or nine finally has the coordination and ability to use the many different mental faculties required to play an instrument. Curwen (and Miss Mason) believed it best to wait until at least age eight because small fingers and lack of coordination will cause younger children to develop poor habits that have to be undone later on. Curwen says:

> There have been instances, yes; but these are isolated cases of genius, which do not apply to the average child. A few simple experiments in imitating hand and finger movements will prove to any parent that the average child of seven or eight has a great deal more motor control than the average child of five. The movement which is made easily by the one is impossible for the other. . . . Yet to do all this at five years old is, *psycho*logically and physiologically, an impossibility. What is the teacher to do? Either to blame and punish the child for not doing that which he is unable to do, thereby inflicting on him grave moral injury, or to be content with wrong positions and movements which soon become habits, and are only cured in after years at the cost of much trouble and discouragement. Pianoforte playing is only one department of musical education. If the years up to seven or even eight are well filled with musical experiences, first through rote-singing and then note-singing, the time is not lost, and the opening intelligence of the second period of childhood is better able to cope with the complexities of instrumental work.[122]

A few hints, paraphrased from Curwen:

> 1) If the child is to play beautifully with good technique, the teacher must also play beautifully with good technique. Children are fantastic imitators. They will imitate the good and the bad.

> 2) As soon as the student is able to read them, finger exercises should be mastered and memorized.

3) Some of the greatest musicians could fit all of their exercises onto one page of sheet music. No more than six exercises, "each with a different and a definite aim," are necessary to develop strong technique—so long as each exercise is "memorized, made perfect in its slow form, and gradually developed in speed, or force, or delicacy, according to its object."[123]

A final word to the wise from Curwen:

One of the fundamental mistakes in pianoforte teaching has been that only one sense was appealed to, and that the wrong one. Music reaches heart and brain through the ear, yet we have usually tried to teach it through the eye. It was always "look," and never "listen." Children were introduced to notation before they had consciously observed any of the musical phenomena which the notation symbolizes.

Every lesson from the very beginning should contain two parts: something to remember and something to do: theory and practice.

Though everything else may appear shallow and repulsive, even the smallest task in music is so absorbing, and carries us so far away from town, country, earth, and all worldly things, that it is truly a blessed gift of God.

—Felix Mendelssohn

Appendix A

Charlotte Mason's Original Programmes for Music Study

YEAR 1

MUSIC APPRECIATION (V. 2)

Listen to music by three composers:

Schumann

Grieg

Brahms

Singing (v. 2)

1. Six French songs:

   French Songs by Violet Partington or

   French Rounds and Nursery Rhymes or

   Sonnez les Matinees

2. Two hymns and a Christmas carol

3. The Joyous Book of Singing Games by John Hornby or Songtime,
   ed. by Percy Dearmer

Music (v. 2)

Learn to play the piano, using The Child Pianist.

Year 2

Music Appreciation (v. 2)

Listen to music by three composers:

Debussy

Schubert

Wagner

(Stories from Wagner by J.W. McSpadden may be used.)

Singing (v. 2)

1. Six French songs:

French Songs by Violet Partington or

French Rounds and Nursery Rhymes or

Sonnez les Matinees

2. Two hymns and a Christmas carol

3. Six English songs from The National Songbook, ed. by C.V. Stanford

4. Ten Minutes' Lessons in Sight-singing

lessons 1-6

lessons 7-11

lessons 12-15

Music (v. 2)

Learn to play the piano, using The Child Pianist.

YEAR 3

MUSIC APPRECIATION (V. 2)

Listen to music by three composers:

Mussorgsky & Borodin

Handel

Dvorak

Singing (v. 2)

1. Six French songs:

French Songs by Violet Partington or

French Rounds and Nursery Rhymes or

Sonnez les Matinees

2. Two hymns and a Christmas carol

3. Six English songs from The National Songbook, ed. by C.V. Stanford

4. Ten Minutes' Lessons in Sight-singing:

lessons 16-19

lessons 20-23

lessons 24-27

Music (v. 2)

Learn to play the piano, using The Child Pianist.

YEAR 4

MUSIC APPRECIATION (V. 2)

Listen to music by three composers:

Mendelssohn

Bach

Beethoven

Optional:

The Book of the Great Musicians by P. Scholes

Singing (v. 2)

1. Six to nine French songs

   A Book of French Songs or

   Voyez Comme on Danse[124]

2. Six English songs from The National Songbook, ed. by C.V. Stanford

3. Learn songs by the composers studied in Music Appreciation and
   Christmas carols when appropriate.

4. Fifty Steps in Sight-singing: Exercises for Pupils, by Arthur Somervell

   steps 1-4

   steps 5-10

   steps 11-12

For reference:

Ten Minutes' Lessons in Sight-singing

   lessons 12-19

   lessons 20-23

   lessons 24-27

Music (v. 2)

Learn to play the piano, using The Child Pianist.

YEAR 5

MUSIC APPRECIATION (V. 2)

Listen to music by three composers:

Mozart?

?

?

Optional:

The Book of the Great Musicians by P. Scholes

Singing (v. 2)

1. Six to nine French songs

   A Book of French Songs or

   Voyez Comme on Danse

2. Six English songs from The National Songbook, ed. by C.V. Stanford

3. Learn songs by the composers studied in Music Appreciation and Christmas carols when appropriate.

4. Fifty Steps in Sight-singing: Exercises for Pupils, by Arthur Somervell

   steps 13-16

   steps 17-18

   steps 19-20

For reference:

Ten Minutes' Lessons in Sight-singing

   lessons 28-34

   lessons 35-37

   lessons 41, 43

Music (v. 2)

Learn to play the piano, using The Child Pianist.

YEAR 6

MUSIC APPRECIATION (V. 2)

Listen to music by three composers:

  Chopin

  Haydn

  Schubert

Optional:

  The Book of the Great Musicians by P. Scholes

Singing (v. 2)

  1. Six to nine French songs

    A Book of French Songs or

    Voyez Comme on Danse

  2. Six English songs from The National Songbook, ed. by C.V. Stanford

  3. Learn songs by the composers studied in Music Appreciation and
    Christmas carols when appropriate.

  4. Fifty Steps in Sight-singing: Eexercises for Pupils, by ArthurSomervell

    steps 21-26

    steps 27-32

    steps 33-34

For reference:

  Ten Minutes' Lessons in Sight-singing

    lessons 38, 40, 42, 44

    lesson 45

    lessons 46-49

Music (v. 2)

  Learn to play the piano, using The Child Pianist.

YEAR 7

MUSIC APPRECIATION (V. 2)

Listen to music by three composers:

Wagner

Purcell

Debussy

The Listener's Guide to Music by P. Scholes

Musical Groundwork by F.H. Shera

Singing (v. 2)

1. Nine French songs

   French songs, with music or

   La Lyre des Ecoles

2. Nine German songs

   Deutscher Liedergarten

3. Nine English songs

   The National Songbook, ed. by C.V. Stanford

4. Learn songs by the composers studied in Music Appreciation and

   Christmas carols when appropriate.

5. Fifty Steps in Sight-singing: Exercises for Pupils, by Arthur Somervell

   steps 35-38

   steps 39-40

   steps 41, 43

For reference:

Ten Minutes' Lessons in Sight-singing

   lessons 50-52, etc.

Music (v. 2)

Choose and learn a suitable composition from the programme of
music each term.

YEAR 8

MUSIC APPRECIATION (V. 2)

Listen to music by three composers:

Handel

Tchaikovsky

Bach

The Listener's Guide to Music by P. Scholes

Optional:

The Second Book of Great Musicians by P. Scholes

Singing (v. 2)

1. Nine French songs

French songs, with music or

La Lyre des Ecoles

2. Nine German songs

Deutscher Liedergarten

3. Nine English songs

The National Songbook, ed. by C.V. Stanford

4. Learn songs by the composers studied in Music Appreciation and Christmas carols when appropriate.

5. Fifty Steps in Sight-singing: Exercises for Pupils, by Arthur Somervell

steps 44-46

steps 47-50

For reference:

Ten Minutes' Lessons in Sight-singing

Music (v. 2)

Choose and learn a suitable composition from the programme of music each term.

YEAR 9

MUSIC APPRECIATION (V. 2)

Listen to music by three composers:

Beethoven

Mendelssohn

Franck

The Listener's Guide to Music by P. Scholes

Optional:

The Second Book of Great Musicians by P. Scholes

Singing (v. 2)

1. Nine French songs

French songs, with music or

La Lyre des Ecoles

2. Nine German songs

Deutscher Liedergarten

3. Nine English songs

The National Songbook, ed. by C.V. Stanford

4. Learn songs by the composers studied in Music Appreciation and

Christmas carols when appropriate.

5. Musical Groundwork by F.H. Shera

term 1

term 2

term 3

Music (v. 2)

Choose and learn a suitable composition from the programme of music each term.

YEAR 10

MUSIC APPRECIATION (V. 2)

Listen to music by three composers:

    Mozart

    Chopin + (optional) Chopin by J.C. Hadden

    Schumann

Optional:

    The Enjoyment of Music by A.W. Pollitt

    Lives of the Great Composers, ed. by A.L. Bacharach

    The Musical Companion, ed. by A.L. Bacharach

Singing (v. 2)

    Six French songs

    Six German or Italian songs

    Six English songs

    Learn songs by the composers studied in Music Appreciation and
    Christmas carols when appropriate.

    Clarendon Song Books, books V & VI

    Oxford Book of Carols

    Clarendon Classical Song Books, Book I

    Clarendon Aria Books, Book I

    Practical Sight-singer, by A. Carse

    term 3 only: Album of 30 Songs, by Schumann

Music (v. 2)

    Choose and learn suitable compositions from the programme of music
    each term.

Optional:

    The Growth of Music by H.C. Colles

    Foundations of Practical Harmony and Counterpoint, by R.O. Morris

    -12 chapters; see preface or Practical Harmony, by Stewart Macpherson

    Elements of Music, by F. Davenport

YEAR 11

MUSIC APPRECIATION (V. 2)

Listen to music by three composers:

    Brahms

    Dvorak

    Haydn

    optional:

    The Enjoyment of Music, by A.W. Pollitt

    Lives of the Great Composers, ed. by A.L. Bacharach

    The Musical Companion, ed. by A.L. Bacharach

Singing (v. 2)

    Six French songs

    Six German or Italian songs

    Six English songs

    Learn songs by the composers studied in Music appreciation and
    Christmas carols when appropriate.

    Clarendon Song Books, Books V & VI

    Oxford Book of Carols

    Clarendon Classical Song Books, Book I

    Clarendon Aria Books, Book I

    Practical Sight-singer, by A. Carse

Music (v. 2)

    Choose and learn suitable compositions from the programme of music
    each term.

Optional:

    The Growth of Music, by H.C. Colles

    Foundations of Practical Harmony and Counterpoint, by R.O. Morris
    -12 chapters; see preface or Practical Harmony, by Stewart Macpherson

    Elements of Music, by F. Davenport

YEAR 12

MUSIC APPRECIATION (V. 2)

Listen to music by three composers:

Elgar

Purcell

Handel

Optional:

The Enjoyment of Music, by A.W. Pollitt

Lives of the Great Composers, ed. by A.L. Bacharach

The Musical Companion, ed. by A.L. Bacharach

Music (v. 2)

Choose and learn suitable compositions by:

Bach, Handel, Haydn, Mozart or Beethoven, Schubert, Chopin, Schumann

no room: Brahms, Franck, Tchaikovsky, Elgar

Optional:

The Growth of Music, by H.C. Colles

book I

book II

book III

For reference:

Clarendon Song Books, Books V-VI

Oxford Book of Carols

Appendix B

Art and Literature—Three Years' Course

Selected by Marjorie Ransom, former student at the House of Education, Ambleside

FIRST YEAR: AGE 8 OR 9

CLASS I A - JANUARY (FOUR MONTHS)
Mendelssohn
Van Dyck
Folk Songs
Dancing

CLASS I B - MAY (FOUR MONTHS)
Purcell
Fra Angelica
French and English Songs
Dancing

CLASS I B - SEPTEMBER (FOUR MONTHS)
Handel
Matthew Maris
French and English Songs
Dancing
Two Hymns by Wesley
Master of Musicians by Emma Marshall

SECOND YEAR: AGE 9 OR 10

CLASS II B - JANUARY (FOUR MONTHS)
Bach
Constable
French Songs
Dancing
English Songs
Two Hymns by Cowper
Campbell's Songs and Ballads

CLASS II B - MAY (FOUR MONTHS)
Mozart
Millet
Songs
Dancing
Hymns by Keble

CLASS II A - SEPTEMBER (FOUR MONTHS)
Beethoven
Watts
French and English Songs
Dancing
Two Hymns by Wesley
Master of Musicians by Emma Marshall

THIRD YEAR: AGE 11 OR 12

CLASS III A - JANUARY (FOUR MONTHS)
Schumann
Jan Steen and Gerard Dow
French and English Songs
Dancing

MAY (FOUR MONTHS)
Grieg
Corot
French and English Songs
Dancing

SEPTEMBER TO DECEMBER (FOUR MONTHS)
Brahms
Durer
French and English Songs
Dancing
Excerpted from the article "Art and Literature in the Parents' Union School," *Parents' Review* vol. 34 (1923), pp. 75–84.

Appendix C

Useful Websites

The Baby's Bouquet
http://www.gutenberg.org/files/25432/25432-h/25432-h.htm

The Baby's Opera
http://www.gutenberg.org/files/25418/25418-h/25418-h.htm

Tribute to Olive Dame Campbell:
http://blog.folkschool.org/2015/07/06/a-tribute-to-olive-dame-camp-bell-1882-1954/

http://www.live365.com/genres/classical

http://www.classicalconnect.com

http://theclassicalstation.org

http://www.classical.com/home

http://www.sky.fm/classical/

http://classicalwebcast.com

http://tunein.com/radio/Classical-c57939/

http://theclassicalstation.org/internet.shtml

http://www.pandora.com/music/classical/classical

http://www.weta.org/fm/listenlive

http://classical-music-online.net

http://www.last.fm/tag/classical

How to read guitar music notes:
   http://www.yourguitarsage.com/wp-content/uploads/2012/05/

   How-To-Read-Guitar-Music-Notes.pdf

Free piano lessons:
   http://www.pianomother.com/piano_lessons.html

How to read music:
   http://readsheetmusic.info/readingmusic.shtml

How to read music (easier):
   http://teoria.com/tutorials/reading/12-notes.php

Composers by Time Period:
   http://www.classical-composers.org/page/period

100 Best Composers:
   http://www.digitaldreamdoor.com/pages/best-classic-comp.html

Top 10 Composers:
   http://writewhat.com/best-composers-ever/

Mendelssohn's Elijah:
   https://www.youtube.com/watch?v=H3ACAdK9MDQ:

Chopin's Nocturne:
   https://www.youtube.com/watch?v=EP8MW6WE9R4

Massenet's Meditation from Thais:
   https://www.youtube.com/watch?v=luL1T1WQC2k

All of Puccini's *Tosca*:
   https://www.youtube.com/watch?v=hxdiJ74AL5Y

Nessun Dorma from *Turandot*:
   https://www.youtube.com/watch?v=VATmgtmR5o4

Beethoven's Romance No. 2 in F:
https://www.youtube.com/watch?v=P0YCWZnpoO0

Beethoven's Moonlight Sonata:
https://www.youtube.com/watch?v=4Tr0otuiQuU

Edvard Grieg's Peer Gynt:
https://www.youtube.com/watch?v=dyM2AnA96yE

Offenbach's Barcarolle from *Tales of Hoffman*:
https://www.youtube.com/watch?v=3DVkGTbIBR0

Prokofiev's Romeo and Juliet:
https://www.youtube.com/watch?v=coxgnE3aTs0

Franz Liszt's Liebestraum:
https://www.youtube.com/watch?v=KpOtuoHL45Y

Liszt's Hungarian Rhapsody:
https://www.youtube.com/watch?v=0odaG9qi818

Mussorgsky's Night on Bald Mountain:
https://www.youtube.com/watch?v=iCEDfZgDPS8

Hodie Natus Est:
https://www.youtube.com/watch?v=dxqm8S-O1T0

Frank's Panis Angelicus:
https://www.youtube.com/watch?v=ocXCtgJD1qM

Tchaikovsky's Romeo and Juliet:
https://www.youtube.com/watch?v=_2jKeYuPvjM

Rimsky-Korsakov's Scheherezade:
https://www.youtube.com/watch?v=SQNymNaTr-Y

Faure's Sicilienne:
https://www.youtube.com/watch?v=MUj7NgFHYB0

Any guitar music performed by Andres Segovia or John Williams:
https://www.youtube.com/watch?v=MuiwZOqmxB0

https://www.youtube.com/watch?v=wW6DTw-4Ulw

Music Downloads from the Isabella Gardner Museum
http://www.gardnermuseum.org/music/listen/podcasts

Boston Symphony
https://www.bso.org/brands/bso/education-community/students-
educators/bso-youth-concerts/teacher-resources.aspx

New York Philharmonic
http://nyphil.org/education/learning-communities/teacherresources

Music Memory
http://www.knowledgeadventure.com/games/music-memory/

DSO Lesson Plan Database
http://www.dsokids.com/resources/lesson-plan-database.aspx

DSO Kids Listening by Composer
http://www.dsokids.comwww.dsokids.com/

Kids Classical Channel
http://www.wgbh.org/kids/kids_classical.cfm?

Classics for Kids
http://www.classicsforkids.com/parents/

Learn the Instruments of the Orchestra
http://artsedge.kennedy-center.org/interactives/perfectpitch/

From the Top
http://www.fromthetop.org/

Kids Music Corner
http://kidsmusiccorner.co.uk/

Make Your Own Instruments
   http://www.dariamusic.com/crafts.php

Young Person's Guide to the Orchestra
   http://listeningadventures.carnegiehall.org/index.aspx

In Depth Learning Activities for Dvorak's New World Symphony
   http://www.carnegiehall.org/Article.aspx?id=4294972158

Curriculum Materials from Carnegie Hall
   http://www.carnegiehall.org/DigitalLibrary/ListView/

Appendix D

Recommended Reading

(Books Charlotte Mason Used)

- *The Baby's Bouquet*
- *The Baby's Opera*
- *Master of Musicians* by Emma Marshall
- *Listener's Guide to Music* by Alfred Scholes
- *Studies of the Great Composers* by Sir Hubert Parry
- *The Enjoyment of Music* by Arthur W Pollitt
- *An Introduction to Music* by H. E. Piggott
- *The Term's Music* by Cedric Howard Glover
- *Musical Groundwork* by Mr. Frank Henry Shera
- *Elements of Music* by F. Davenport
- *The Teacher's Guide to The Pianoforte Method/The Pianoforte Method* by Annie Jessy Curwen
- *Fifty Steps in Sight-Singing* by Arthur Somervell
- *Story Lives of Master Musicians* by Harriette Brower
- *Foundations of Practical Harmony and Counterpoint* by R. O. Morris
- *The Oxford Song Book*

Appendix E

English Folk Songs[125]

- Adieu Sweet Lovely Nancy
- All Around My Hat
- Barbara Allen
- Barrack Street
- Blackwaterside
- Blaydon Races
- Blow Boys Blow
- Blow the Man Down
- The Blue Cockade
- Bobby Shafto
- Drink to Me Only With Thine Eyes (To Celia)
- Drunken Sailor
- Early One Morning
- English Country Garden
- The Flandyke Shore
- The Foggy Dew
- Fountains Flowing (Our Captain Calls All Hands)
- The Girl I Left Behind (Brighton Camp)
- The Grand Old Duke of York
- Greensleeves
- Haul Away Joe
- Isle of France
- Jack Hall
- John Barleycorn
- Just as the Tide was Flowing
- Lavender's Blue
- London Bridge is Falling Down
- Lord Bateman
- Lord Franklin
- Maggie May
- Matty Groves (Little Musgrave)
- The Newry Highwayman
- On Ilka Moor Baht'at
- Oranges and Lemons
- The Riddle Song (I Gave my Love a Cherry)
- Rock-a-Bye Baby
- The Rose of Allendale
- Scarborough Faire
- The Smuggler's Song
- South Australia
- Spanish Ladies
- Spencer the Rover
- Sprig of Thyme
- This Old Man
- Twinkle, Twinkle, Little Star
- When the Boat Comes In (Dance to Your Daddy)

Appendix F

Brief Glossary of Musical Terms

TERMS FOR TEMPOS:

Adagio – slow and stately

Andante – at a walking pace

Andante moderato – between andante and moderato (thus the name andante moderato)

Moderato – moderately

Allegretto – moderately fast

Allegro moderato – close to but not quite allegro

Allegro – fast, quickly, and bright

Vivace – lively and fast

TERMS FOR TEMPO CHANGES:

Ritardando – gradually slowing down

Accelerando – gradually accelerating

Vivace – lively and fast

from https://en.wikipedia.org/wiki/Tempo

TERMS FOR DYNAMICS:

Crescendo: a slow increase in volume. Abbreviated cresc.

Decrescendo: a slow decrease in volume. Abbreviated *decresc.*

Diminuendo: a slow decrease in volume. Abbreviated *dim.*

Forte: loud. Abbreviated *f.*

Fortissimo: extra loud. Abbreviated *ff.*

Pianissimo: extra quiet. Abbreviated *pp.*

Piano: quiet. Abbreviated *p.*

Sforzando: musical instruction that indicates playing a note with sudden force. Abbreviated *sfz.*

Appendix G

Listening Recommendations

(from professional musicians who play each instrument)

From acclaimed violinist Joshua Bell (no, I did not ask him personally—I found this one online):

> *The Brahms Violin Concerto.* He prefers it to more difficult pieces from Paganini.

From Hannah Hoyt, Vocal Performance and Film Scoring graduate, Berklee College of Music, and performer with Opera Carolina:

Ralph Vaughan Williams, The Lark Ascending

Beautiful, lilting birdsong. Interestingly, he began writing this piece shortly before World War I broke out and did not finish it until his tour in France ended. It's far more beautiful and haunting when placed within the backdrop of war. Twinges of sadness and devastation come through.

https://www.youtube.com/watch?v=OLhpkvQLDt0

Max Bruch, Violin Concerto in G minor

This is a famous standard for violin repertoire and used in more dramatic film scores.

https://www.youtube.com/watch?v=UxZbVwrGOrc

Antonio Vivaldi, A Minor Concerto for Two Violins (first and second movements especially)

Vivaldi was the first known violin virtuoso, and this is an important piece of historic significance.

https://www.youtube.com/watch?v=Z3OhLrTeiMQ

Nicolo Paganini, Caprice 24 and La Campanella

Paganini performed so well that people said he must have gotten his talent by selling his soul to the devil. He was the most famous violinist of his time, and perhaps of all time.

Caprice 24
https://www.youtube.com/watch?v=YCsVEsQlm7o

La Campanella
https://www.youtube.com/watch?v=0OY2-83CT1g

Johann Sebastian Bach, Concerto in D Minor (known as The Bach Double)

https://www.youtube.com/watch?v=DJh6i-t_I1Q

Mendelssohn, Violin Concerto in E Minor (first movement)

This is probably the most well-known and difficult piece in the violinist's repertoire, and it is always an audience favorite.

https://www.youtube.com/watch?v=Pmj7nCRYNs4

"The Germans have four violin concertos. The greatest, most uncompromising is Beethoven's. The one by Brahms vies with it in seriousness. The richest, the most seductive, was written by Max Bruch. But the most inward, the heart's jewel, is Mendelssohn's."
-Joseph Joachim

From Maestro James Meena, Director of Opera Carolina:

Mozart, "Non più andrai" from The *Marriage of Figaro*. "One of the most perfect pieces of music ever written. The recurring main theme makes this aria like a rondo, which is a traditional form that finishes sonatas – often piano sonatas by Mozart and Beethoven."

Verdi, "O patria mia" from *Aida*. "The most heartfelt expression of loss of country. Verdi's writing for the oboe, accompanying the soprano, is sublime."

Wagner, "*Wintersturme*" from *Die Walkyre*. "The greatest expression of love, nature and springtime ever written."

Wagner, "*Liedestod*" from *Tristan und Isolde*. "A difficult piece to approach, but one has to read the text and then imagine Isolde's expression of love for the fallen Tristan."

Puccini, "Ch'ella mi creda" from *La Fanciulla del West*. "Puccini at his best."

Carlisle Floyd, "The Trees on the Mountain" from *Susannah*. "Simply one of the finest opera arias written in the latter part of the 20th century."

From Joann Falletta, Music Director of the Buffalo Philharmonic and The Virginia Symphony:

"Children respond positively to music selections that tell a story."
Prokofiev, *Peter and the Wolf*.
Poulenc, *Babar the Elephant*.
Britten, *Young Person's Guide to the Orchestra*.
Dukas, *The Sorcerer's Apprentice*.
Ott, *The Thrill of the Orchestra*.
Ravel, *Mother Goose Suite*.
Saint-Saëns, *Carnival of the Animals*.

From Elizabeth Richter, Professor of Harp at Ball State University:

Handel, *Concerto in Bb*. "Baroque, lively first and third movements, stately second movement, catchy and rhythmic themes. About 10 minutes. One of the earliest pieces written for the modern harp."

Ravel, *Introduction and Allegro*. "Gorgeous piece for harp, strings, flute and clarinet. Full of lush harmonies and has a wonderful cadenza in the middle."

Salzedo, *Chanson dans la Nuit*. "Exotic 20th century work that includes a lot of special sound effects such as tapping the sound board and playing with fingernails."

Professional bassoonist and home educator Jessi Vandagriff collected woodwind selections from a variety of musicians.

First, from Amber Seeley, MM, for flute:

Honegger, *Danse de la chèvre*. "Unaccompanied flute. At the beginning of the piece, the low notes of the flute are showcased. It then moves on to a fast passage that shows how many notes flute players can play in a row. Near the end of the piece, the slow, low note part comes back. See if you can hear it."

https://www.youtube.com/watch?v=L0oFwAH07mw

Mozart's flute and harp concerto. "You can get info about this online, it's a really well known piece."

Smetana, *The Moldau*. "The first full minute of the piece is a flute duet that represents the flowing waters of the Moldau River. (The rest of the piece is good too, but this beginning is a great example of flute playing in an orchestra, more info available online)" https://www.youtube.com/watch?v=3G4NKzmfC-Q

From Jessi Vandagriff, Professor of Bassoon, Brigham Young University, Idaho, for Bassoon:

Saint-Saëns, *Sonata for Bassoon and Piano.* "Most bassoonists consider this the most beautiful piece ever written for bassoon. It was the final piece the great composer Camille Saint-Saëns ever wrote."

https://www.youtube.com/watch?v=1Wop1u7-K9s part 1

https://www.youtube.com/watch?v=woMvkisAqvE part 2

Carl Maria von Weber, Andante and Hungarian Rondo. "This piece begins with a slow, sad section. It continues to pick up momentum until, at the end of the rondo, the bassoonist is playing notes that are incredibly fast! Each note starts with the tongue. Try to say ta-ta-ta-ta along with the notes. Can you keep up?"

https://www.youtube.com/watch?v=VOfyw_G7jsg

In the Hall of the Mountain King or The Sorcerer's Apprentice. "Both great examples of the bassoon's use in the orchestra."

From Jory Woodis, Megan Fisher, and Chris Wilson for saxophone:

Paul Bonneau, *Caprice en forme de valse.* "This in an unaccompanied piece for saxophone. It is fun and shows how the saxophone can jump around to play in different octaves. This is an example of classical saxophone music."

https://www.youtube.com/watch?v=Fe4QCxOYrOs

Paule Marice, "Tableau de Provence." "This is one of the most well-loved classical saxophone pieces. The saxophone was invented in France and much of its classical music was written by French composers."

https://www.youtube.com/watch?v=9cLyFAl_Oqw

John Williams, *Escapades: I. Closing In* (From the movie *Catch Me If You Can*). "The saxophone is usually associated with jazz and popular music. This piece is a good example of how classical music and jazz can be combined into one piece."

https://www.youtube.com/watch?v=VEKz0AlKTLY

From Megan Miller, MM, oboe teacher from Pleasant Grove, Utah:

Mozart, Oboe Quartet in F Major, K. 370 (first movement)

https://www.youtube.com/watch?v=Gu87qUExo9c

Ralph Vaughan Williams, Oboe Concerto (first movement - Rondo Pastorale)

https://www.youtube.com/watch?v=LCJu4eNdMxY

Hamilton Harty, "Chansonette"

https://www.youtube.com/watch?v=bkIinN-Rrns

Clarinet players Hannah Christensen, MM, Vanessa Young, and Andrea Butler recommend:

Mozart, *Clarinet Concerto*. "This is one of Mozart's most well-known concertos. The clarinet was invented later than the other woodwind instruments. Mozart was one of the first composers to use it extensively. His love for the instrument is apparent in this concerto."

https://www.youtube.com/watch?v=o_gm0NCabPs

Astor Piazzolla, *Tango Etude No. 3*. "Unaccompanied clarinet. Clarinetists often play music that wasn't originally written for clarinet. This is one of those examples. It is an arrangement of a South American tango written by Argentinian composer Astor Piazzolla."

https://www.youtube.com/watch?v=ldw2uD9A5cE

Gounod, *Funeral March of a Marionette*. "The main theme of this piece is played by a clarinet. It is joined by another clarinet and two bassoons to make this song sound a little spooky. It is frequently programmed during the Halloween season."

https://www.youtube.com/watch?v=zH7nXgzKpM0

"For something a little jazzy, Joseph Horovitz' *Sonatina for clarinet and piano* is fun."

"We loved theme and variations, so *Carnival of Venice* is fun."

Carl Stamitz clarinet concerto is also great, as is Finzi's *Five Bagatelles*."

English Horn:

Dvorak, *New World Symphony*. "Second movement is probably the best intro to the English horn."

"There is an arrangement of Ravel's *Pavane for a Dead Princess* which is nice."
http://www.carolynhovemusic.com/recordings/

Appendix H

Charlotte Mason's Trusted Music Advisors

PERCY ALFRED SCHOLES

Percy Scholes was best known for his book *The Oxford Companion to Music*. He wrote this exhaustive volume of over a million words over the course of six years, and it was his magnum opus. Charlotte Mason used his *Listener's Guide to Music* in her programmes, probably because the *Oxford Companion* was not yet available, since he completed it in 1938. Scholes was born in 1877 and died in 1958.

EMMA MARSHALL

Emma Marshall formed an attachment to Henry Wadsworth Longfellow after reading his poem "Evangeline." They wrote back and forth for years and he undoubtedly influenced her choice of career. She wrote many books for children, including *Master of the Musicians: A Tale of Handel's Days*, *Alma: The Story of a Little Music Mistress*, and *In the Choir of Westminster Abbey: A Story of Henry Purcell's Days*, along with dozens of other works. She was a prolific children's writer whose work would have been well known by Charlotte Mason.

HUBERT PARRY

Hubert Parry was a contributor to *Grove's Dictionary of Music and Musicians*, head of the Royal College of Music, professor of music at the University of Oxford, an author of books about music, and a composer in his own right. Some considered him as great an English composer as Henry Purcell, and Edward Elgar said he learned much about music from Parry's articles in *Grove's Dictionary*. Ralph Vaughan Williams studied under Parry at the Royal College of Music. While he was a trusted mentor to many, critics gave mixed reviews of his compositions.

MRS. HOWARD GLOVER
AND HER SON, CEDRIC HOWARD GLOVER

Mrs. Howard Glover originally wrote to the *Parents' Review* urging that children's musical education should not be limited to their own efforts at learning an instrument, but that they should be trained to hear and enjoy music, to become good listeners. Charlotte Mason induced her to prepare a program of composers' work each term, and her son Cedric continued this helpful activity. He also arranged that PNEU schools should meet and sing together and have their orchestras compete against each other in a friendly competition.

ANNIE JESSY CURWEN

Annie Curwen was a piano teacher in Dublin until she moved to Scotland and met famed music educator John Curwen, who was promoting the tonic sol-fa method at the time. She adapted the method for piano. Annie married John Curwen's son John Spencer Curwen and published several books, under her married name Mrs. Spencer Curwen, for her father-in-law's publishing company. Her most prominent book was *Mrs. Curwen's Pianoforte Method (The Child Pianist): Being a Practical Course of the Elements of Music.* Around twenty editions were published, along with a *Teacher's Guide* for each edition. She originally wrote the book for her own children, creating exercises and duets that she composed for them.

ARTHUR SOMERVELL

Arthur Somervell was an English composer of art song who wrote choral works and song cycles in religious and secular settings. He was influenced by Mendelssohn and Brahms. In 1920, he was made Principal Inspector of Music for the Board of Education. Like Hubert Parry, he was professor of music at the Royal College of Music. He was also a conductor.

HARRIETTE BROWER

During Miss Mason's time, Harriette Brower wrote many, many books on piano and vocal mastery, composers, and more. Here are a few: *Modern Masters of the Keyboard; Piano Mastery: Talks with Master Pianists and Teachers; Vocal Mastery: Talks with Master Singers and Teachers, Comprising Interviews with Caruso, Farrar, Maurel, Lehmann, and Others; The World's Great Men of Music* (also published as *Story-Lives of Master Musicians*); and *The Art of the Pianist: Technic and Poetry in Piano Playing, for Teacher and Student.*

R. O. MORRIS

Reginald Owen Morris was a British composer, born in York and educated at the Royal College of Music. He became a professor of counterpoint and composition and wrote many counterpoint textbooks. He married Emmie Fisher, whose sister Adeline was married to Ralph Vaughan Williams, thus making the famous composer his brother-in-law.

Charlotte Mason's Close Friends and Associates at the PNEU

ELSIE KITCHING was Miss Mason's great friend and upon her death, Mrs. Kitching was given oversight of the mission of the PNEU, as its director.

MRS. HENRIETTE FRANKLIN was the Hon. Secretary of the PNEU and Chairman of the Charlotte Mason Foundation.

MRS. EMELINE STEINTHAL was a co-founder of the PNEU and brought Miss Mason's principles to a Yorkshire mining village.

MR. HORACE HOUSEHOLD was Secretary for Education for Gloucestershire and a great friend to the PNEU, having introduced her principles at five schools and seeing what the Parents' Union Schools provided to their children.

Bibliographic Notes

1. Charlotte M. Mason, *School Education* (London: Kegan Paul, Trench, Trübner, 1905) p. 188.
2. Cedric Howard Glover, *The Term's Music*, (London: Kegan Paul, Trench, Trubner & Co., Ltd., 1925).
3. Cedric Howard Glover, *The Term's Music*, pp 5-6.
4. H. W. Household, "A Liberal Education in Secondary Schools 1-12," *The Parent's Review*, Volume 31, no. 3, (March 1920).
5. May Byron, *A Day With Ludwig Van Beethoven* (New York: Hodder & Stoughton, n.d.).
6. "Fanny Crosby." Bible.org. n.p., n.d.
7. Charlotte M. Mason, *Parents and Children* (London: K. Paul, Trench, Trübner, 1897) p. 271.
8. Ibid, p. 20.
9. Ibid, p 199.
10. http://maudpowell.org/home/ForYoungPeople/TheAmericanGirlViolin tabid/112/Default.aspx
11. Cedric Howard Glover, *The Term's Music*, pp. 5-6.
12. Ibid.
13. https://www.amblesideonline.org/PR/PR09p439MusicTeaching.shtml
14. Charlotte M. Mason, *Parents and Children*, p 185.
15. Charlotte M Mason, *Ourselves* (London: K. Paul, Trench, Trübner, 1897), p. 30.
16. http://www.dailygood.org/story/545/the-last-quiet-place-krista-tippett/
17. https://www.amblesideonline.org/PR/PR09p439MusicTeaching.shtml
18. Charlotte M. Mason, *Home Education: A Course of Lectures to Ladies*, Delivered in Bradford, in the Winter of 1885-1886. (London: K. Paul, Trench, 1886) p. 315.
19. Annie Jessy Curwen, *The Teacher's Guide to Mrs. Curwen's Pianoforte Method* (London, England: J Curwen & Sons, 1886), p. 1.
20. Charlotte M Mason, *Ourselves*.
21. https://www.amblesideonline.org/PR/PR09p439MusicTeaching.shtml
22. Ibid.
23. Ibid.

24. Marjorie Ransom, "Art and Literature in the Parents' Union School," *Parents' Review*, Volume 34, 1923, pgs 75-84.

25. Cedric Howard Glover, *The Term's Music*, p. 40.

26. Mrs. Davenport, "On Piano Playing," *Parents' Review*, searchable at www.amblesideonline.org.

27. Percy A. Scholes, *The Listener's Guide to Music*, with a Concert-goer's Glossary (London: H. Milford, 1922).

28. Ibid.

29. Ibid.

30. Ibid.

31. *Young Person's Guide to the Orchestra* by Benjamin Britten https://www.youtube.com/watch?v=4vbvhU22uAM
    A Child's Introduction to the Orchestra and all its Instruments https://childrensvinyl.wordpress.com/2012/07/08/a-childs-introduction-to-the-orchestra/

32. Percy A. Scholes, *The Listener's Guide to Music*.

33. Lucy Lillie, *The Story of Music and Musicians for Young Readers* (New York: Harper & Brothers, 1886), p. 41.

34. Percy A. Scholes, *The Listener's Guide to Music*.

35. Percy A. Scholes, *The First Book of the Great Musicians: A Course in Appreciation for Young Readers* (London: Humphrey Milford Oxford University Press, 1922), pp 7-8.

36. Ibid.

37. Op Cit, pp. 12-13.

38. Tone painting: the use of varying timbres and sound symbolism in creating musical effects, especially in impressionistic composition or program music.

39. http://www.public-domain-content.com/books/beethoven/8.shtml

40. http://www.laphil.com/philpedia/music/ride-of-valkyries-from-die-walkure-richard-wagner

41. Edward Gold, http://www.egoldmidincd.com/program_music.html

42. H. W. Household, "Charlotte Mason and the Nation's Children," *In Memoriam: Charlotte M. Mason* (London: *Parents' Review*, vol. 34, 1923) p. 182.

43. Charlotte M. Mason, *Parents and Children*, p. 82.

44. © Jane Yolen, 2016.

45. http://www.dailygood.org/story/545/the-last-quiet-place-krista-tippett/

46. http://www.dailygood.org/story/545/the-last-quiet-place-krista-tippett/

47. May Byron, *A Day With Ludwig Van Beethoven*.

48. Percy A Scholes, *The First Book of the Great Musicians*, p. 73.

49. Brian Wise, "WQXR - New York's Classical Music Radio Station" (WQXR - New York's Classical Music Radio Station. N.p., n.d. Web. 20 Aug. 2015).

50. Lucy Cecil Lillie, *The Story of Music and Musicians for Young Readers*, p. 141.

51. Brian Wise, "WQXR - New York's Classical Music Radio Station."

52. Ibid.

53. Ibid.

54. Ibid.

55. Lucy Cecil Lillie, *The Story of Music and Musicians for Young Readers*, p. 35.

56. Charlotte M Mason, *Ourselves*, p. 30.

57. David Kettle, "Classical Connections: The Bird's the Word," July 2013 www.sinfinimusic.com/uk/features/series/classical-connections/birdsong#

58. Ibid.

59. Ibid.

60. http://poetsgraves.co.uk/Classic%20Poems/Shelley/ode_to_a_skylark.htm

61. http://jan.ucc.nau.edu/~krr2/ct_nature.html

62. Gretchen Holbrook Gerzina, "100 Years of The Secret Garden," The Public Domain Review. N.p., n.d. Web. 24 Aug. 2015.

63. Emma Pomfret, "Composers' Hideaways: Where do they go?" Sinfinimusic.com, July 2013.

64. Nick Shave, "Music and Nature: Songs of the Sea," Sinfinimusic.com, July 2013.

65. Percy A. Scholes, *The Listener's Guide to Music*, p. 58.

66. Emma Pomfret, "Composers' Hideaways: Where do they go?" Sinfinimusic.com, July 2013.

67. Ibid.

68. "Puccini's Studio at Torre Del Lago," YouTube, n.d. Web, August 2015.

69. Nick Shave, "Music and Nature: Songs of the Sea," Sinfinimusic.com, July 2013.

70. Leon Botstein. "American Symphony Orchestra - Admiration and Emulation: The Friendship of Brahms and Dvořák." American Symphony Orchestra. n.p., n.d. Web. 07 Sept. 2015.

71. May Byron, *A Day With Ludwig Van Beethoven*.

72. C. Hubert H. Parry, Studies of Great Composers, (London: George Routledge and Sons, Ltd., nd).

73. Charlotte M. Mason, *Home Education*, p. 280.

74. "INS Scholarship 1998: The Eroica Riddle: Did Napoleon Remain Beethoven's "Hero?" N.p., n.d. Web. 25 Aug. 2015.

75. Wikipedia. Wikimedia Foundation, n.d. Web. 29 Aug. 2015.

76. https://en.wikipedia.org/wiki/Mozart_and_scatology

77. Danielle Mead Skjelver. "German Hercules: The Impact of Scatology on the Image of Martin Luther as a Man, 1483-1546," University of Maryland, n.d., 07 Sept. 2015.

78. http://www.paganini.com/nicolo/nicindex.htm

79. Alexander Poznansky, "Tchaikovsky: A Life," - Tchaikovsky Research. n.p., n.d. Web. 07 Sept. 2015.

80. Daniel T. Politoske and Martin Werner, "Music," (Prentice Hall, 1988), p. 419.

81. Stephen Walsh, "Stravinsky's Works to 1935", 2000, pp. 543–44.

82. Charlotte M. Mason, *Parents and Children*, p. 186.

83. https://archive.org/details/listenersguideto00schouoft

84. Ross King, *Bruneleschi's Dome* (New York: Penguin Books, 2001).

85. http://bytesdaily.blogspot.com/2011/11/last-words-leonardo-da-vinci.html

86. Percy A Scholes, *The Listener's Guide to Music*, p. 28.

87. http://www.amblesideonline.org/CM/Genesispart1.html

88. https://www.amblesideonline.org/PR/PR08p026PianoTeachers.shtml

89. Cedric Howard Glover, *The Term's Music*.

90. Arthur W. Pollitt, *The Enjoyment of Music* (London: Methuen, n.d.).

91. Charlotte M. Mason, *Home Education: A Course of Lectures to Ladies*, Delivered in Bradford, in the Winter of 1885–1886 (London: K. Paul, Trench, 1886), p. 315.

92. Barbara Davenport, "About Music Teaching," The *Parents' Review*, vol. 14 (1903), pp. 296–99.

93. Charlotte Mason, *Home Education*.

94. Mason, *Parents and Children*, p. 20.

95. http://docslide.net/documents/curwen-tonic-solfa.html

96. Ibid.

97. Available online at http://docslide.net/documents/curwen-tonic-solfa.html.

98. http://www.australian-music-ed.info/Curwen/HistO'view.html

99. Ibid.

100. http://www.philharmonia.co.uk/explore/resources/dictation

101. http://www.loc.gov/resource/ihas.200033206.0/?sp=6

102. Ibid.

103.Ibid.

104.http://www.dailygood.org/story/545/the-last-quiet-place-krista-tippett/

105.http://www.pbs.org/americanrootsmusic/pbs_arm_itc_historical_background.
html

106.https://www.folkschool.org/?section=articles&article_cat_id=&article_id=36

107.http://www.mshumanities.org/pdf/lessons/strumhum.pdf

108.http://spotlightonmusic.macmillanmh.com/n/teachers/articles/folk-and-
traditional-styles/appalachian-folk-music

109.Alan Lomax, "notes for the album," *American Folk Songs for Children*, (Atlantic).

110.http://cuppawithjen.weebly.com/blog/on-folk-music

111.Mrs. Stanton, "The Child Depicted by Poets," The *Parents' Review*, AO *Parents'
Review* Archives, AmblesideOnline.org. n.p., n.d. Web. 07 Sept. 2015.

112.Henry Coward, *Choral Technique and Interpretation* (London: Novello and Co.,
1914).

113. "The Religious Training of Children at Home," *Parents' Review* vol. 3, no. 2
(1892/93).

114.Marjorie Ransom, "Art and Literature in the Parents' Union School," *Parents'
Review*, Volume 34, 1923, pgs 75-84.

115.http://www.dailygood.org/story/545/the-last-quiet-place-krista-tippett/

116.http://www.amblesideonline.org/PR/PR02p038ParentsAndChildren.shtml

117.Charlotte Mason, *Parents and Children*, p. 271.

118.Ibid.

119.Annie Jessy Curwen, *The Teacher's Guide to Mrs. Curwen's Pianoforte Method* (London,
England: J Curwen & Sons, 1886), p. 1.

120.Ibid, p. 2.

121.Ibid.

122.Ibid, p. 3.

123.Ibid., p. 6.

124.http://hdl.handle.net/1802/25411

125.https://www.acousticmusicarchive.com/english-folk-songs-chords-lyrics

Hildegard's Gift

NOW AVAILABLE

Purchase *Hildegard's Gift* at online retail outlets or directly from the publisher at www.paracletepress.com/hildegards-gift.html   Visit our website: www.meganhoyt.net for recipes, coloring sheets, a secret alphabet, and more fun activities for children.

Megan Hoyt offers young readers a glimpse into the life of Hildegard of Bingen. The text is enlivened by artist Hill's bright and whimsical illustrations depicting Hildegard's imaginative life.. **–Publisher's Weekly**

The gifts of Hildegard of Bingen (1098–1179 CE) are not easily translatable into a book for young children. She was a theologian, visionary, poet, and scientist and was renowned for her chants. This picture book serves as a good introduction by bringing the phenomenon down to a child's level. **–Booklist**

Made in the USA
Monee, IL
16 June 2024